CHRIST
The Fullness of the Godhead

A Study in New Testament Christology

CHRIST
The Fullness of the Godhead

"It pleased the Father that in Him should all fullness dwell" (Colossians 1:19)

by
JAMES GUNN

Introduction by Fredk. A. Tatford

LOIZEAUX BROTHERS
Neptune, New Jersey

FIRST EDITION, JANUARY 1983

Library of Congress Cataloging in Publication Data

Gunn, James, 1900-
Christ: the fullness of the godhead

Bibliography: pp. 239-242.
Includes index.
1. Jesus Christ—History of doctrines—Early church, ca. 30-600. 2. Bible. N.T.—Theology. I. Title.
BT198.G85 1982 232 82-17987
ISBN 0-87213-283-8

PRINTED IN THE UNITED STATES OF AMERICA

To

My Daughter Gene

whose love, patience, and understanding

have made these years

so pleasant and productive

CONTENTS

ACKNOWLEDGMENTS

An excellent place to study, to write; shelf upon shelf full of books, books on systematic theology, Bible commentaries, doctrinal dissertations, and expository works in large numbers. Then why is the writing of this book so delayed? By big city distractions: the ringing of the telephone, the front door chimes, the back door buzzer, the door-to-door salesman, etc. Where could one go to be alone with his God, his books, his writing?

What an inspiration! A commitment had been made for one week of ministry at the adult summer conference at Joy Bible Camp. Why not rent a room in the motel and remain there until the end of the season? The arrangement was quickly made.

With a car trunk full of books, an electric typewriter, and other facilities we arrived and quickly set to work in the end room of the motel where others did not need to come.

The atmosphere was clear, the blue sky filled with white fleecy clouds. The gentle lapping of the waves from the lake on the sandy beach, the whispering of the wind through the trees, the singing of the birds all together seemed to produce the relaxation, calmness, and even the urge to continuous research and writing.

One can never forget the brief and helpful daily calls of beloved brother William Belch. Little did we realize that the intimate fellowship of years was to end abruptly in a few months with his going to be with the Lord.

The interest of Gary Pickell was much appreciated. As administrator of the camp he, in passing, would call through the door, "How are things going?"

Mealtime in the dining room had to be reduced somewhat, but each was a delightful experience. The fellowship and enthusiasm of Ernie Belch and his wife Evelyn, and of a host of other friends were strong forces of encouragement.

To all named and unnamed associated with Joy Bible Camp, I tender my sincere thanks.

On returning home there were manuscripts to read, many corrections typographical and otherwise to make. In this tedious task ready voluntary assistance was given by my daughter, Margaret Gene, and her friend, Isobel Telfer. Isobel's expertise as a private secretary proved most helpful. To these two amiable and efficient ladies I am profoundly grateful.

The brief yet pleasant times of fellowship with Dr. Fredk. Tatford are warmly cherished. For his appropriate and scholarly introduction to this whole study I am very, very thankful.

Miss Marie Loizeaux was the first to suggest this work; since the beginning her interest has not declined. From her editorial experience in the publishing field she has willingly given ideas, guidance, and knowledge. To her I do express the most sincere gratitude.

May it please God Himself through these chapters to glorify His Son, Christ—the Fullness of the Godhead. And may the Divine Spirit by the means of this volume take of the things of Christ and reveal them to the readers. This is my fervent prayer.

JAMES GUNN

FOREWORD

The Scripture teaches that it is the Word of God and true in all its parts. It follows that no verse in the Bible can really contradict another, and no verse should be used by itself to prove any doctrine. Instead, all verses on a subject should be considered when a truth is to be stated.

James Gunn, after decades of private study of the Word of God, is well qualified to put together all verses which deal with the subject of Christ. And Christ is the subject of all Scripture, the unifying factor which makes sixty-six books by perhaps forty writers into one Book, properly called the Holy Bible.

The Person and work of our Lord Jesus Christ have consistently been the focal point of satanic attack since the creation. How welcome then, is this comprehensive, thoughtful presentation of the most important doctrines about Christ! It will warm your heart, enlighten your mind, and clarify your thinking about your wonderful Saviour.

All the fullness of the Godhead dwelt bodily in Him.

R.E. HARLOW

INTRODUCTION

Throughout the centuries theologians have sought to crystallize the Biblical teaching concerning the Person of Christ in a concise and accurate statement. But there is probably no better summary of the Church's belief than that contained in Article 11 of the Thirty-Nine Articles, viz.:

> The Son, which is the Word of the Father, begotten from everlasting of the Father, the very and eternal God, and of one substance with the Father, took man's nature in the womb of the Blessed Virgin, of her substance: so that two whole and perfect natures, that is to say, the Godhead and Manhood, were joined together in one Person, never to be divided, whereof is one Christ, very God and very Man, who truly suffered, was crucified, dead and buried, to reconcile His Father to us, and to be a sacrifice, not only for original guilt, but also for all actual sins of men.

This definition is naturally the result of discussion and controversy over a long period, but it represents the general view of evangelical Christians today.

At the inception of Christianity there was a general syncretistic tendency throughout the civilized world. Attempts had been made to harmonize and amalgamate Oriental theosophy, pagan tradition, Hellenistic philosophy, and Judaic thought. Christianity afforded a challenge to the philosopher and logician to absorb a further feature. One direct outcome was the Gnostic teaching which so rapidly spread through Asia Minor even in apostolic days, and to which Colossians, Ephesians, 2 Peter, John, Jude, and the Pastorial Epistles all refer. At the same time, as the Epistle to the Galatians, in particular, plainly indicated, there was also an upsurge of religious legalism, which was directed to the complete Judaizing of Gentile churches. These two opposing tendencies inevitably had their effect upon the Christology of the first two centuries.

The Jewish tendency found its principal expression in Ebionism (a name derived from the Hebrew *byonim,* or poor people, an appropriate description of the Jewish converts of the period). There were two classes of Ebionites. Both combined the observance of the Mosaic law with faith in Christ. The more rigid class insisted that Gentile believers should also observe the law and refused to have fellowship with any who did not, but the more moderate did not regard the law as obligatory upon Gentiles. While the second acknowledged the virgin birth of our Lord, the first declared that He was the Son of Joseph and Mary, but was selected as Messiah because of His exceptional piety. According to this view, His divine selection was revealed at His baptism, and was confirmed to Him by John the Baptist, the power for His mission being imparted at the same time by the descent of the Holy Spirit upon Him. Prior to His baptism He was merely human, but at Jordan the divine nature entered into His life.

The Gnostic philosophy was much more complicated. Gnosticism maintained that matter was inherently evil and that God was infinitely holy, immanent, and incomprehensible. The powers in the divine essence became the germs of life development: the life inherent in them individualized itself in successive emanations from the eternal, each succeeding form being more remote from divinity and possessing less of the divine attributes, until finally a demiurge emerged, who became the framer of the world. The human beings who sprang from the hand of the demiurge, like himself, possessed a small element of divinity, which Jesus, Himself another emanation from God, came to release and thereby to reconcile man to God. This particular heresy was dealt with plainly in the Colossian Epistle, where Paul showed that all the divine attributes in their totality resided in Christ and that the work of creation was His alone.

Cerinthus and other Gnostics taught that Jesus was the son of Joseph and Mary, but that a divine Christ descended upon Him at His baptism, empowered Him throughout His life, and departed from Him at His passion. This implied that there were two Persons—one a heavenly and the other an earthly—in the same body.

Simon Magus (Acts 8:9) was one of the first "Christian" Gnostics. Simon maintained that the body of Jesus was a phantom. This view was adopted in various forms by Basilides, Marcion, Valentinus, the Manichaeans, and others, who thereby acquired the appellation of Docetae (from the Greek verb "appear" or "seem to be"). Some considered that our Lord's entire life was illusory, while others took the view that He was born of Mary, but of ethereal and not material substance. Such teaching was, of course, in direct conflict with the Johannine teaching that the Word "became flesh" (John 1:14), and that Jesus Christ came in the flesh (1 John 4:2; 2 John 7).

Toward the end of the second century there appeared a form of unitarianism, which became known as Monarchianism because its proponents maintained the absolute unity or *monarchia* of the Godhead. There were two main schools of Monarchianism: (1) dynamic and (2) Patripassian or modalistic. The former was represented by leaders such as Paul of Samosata, Theodotus, and Artemon, who denied the incarnation of the Logos and claimed that Jesus was a mere man and that divine power and wisdom were bestowed upon Him at His baptism and operated in Him as in no other man. The leaders of the Patripassian school included Sabellius of Libya, Praxeas, Callistus, and Beryllus. These accepted the divinity of Christ but denied His independent and preexistent personality: His life was only a theophany or transitory manifestation. God was one, and the names—Father, Son, and Holy Spirit—signified no more than different phases in which the divine essence was revealed. The church rejected both forms of the heresy, and the synod of Antioch excommunicated Paul of Samosata in A.D. 268.

Fifty years later trouble broke out at Alexandria, where one of the presbyters named Arius taught that, although He existed before the world, the Logos was not eternal, but was created by God as the first and highest of all His creatures. He argued that the incarnation consisted in the union of the Logos with a human body. Christ was superior to man but inferior to God and was, furthermore, of a different essence. It was upon this last point that the dispute raged hottest. Arianism referred to a similarity but not identity of substance (*homoiousia*), whereas Athanasius and other opponents maintained that the Son was of the same substance (*homoousia*) as the Father and was coexistent and coeternal. Referring to John 1:1-3, William Kelly remarked that it is "impossible to conceive a stronger testimony to His uncreated subsistence, to His distinct personality when He was with God before creation, and to His divine nature. . . . Lest His own consubstantiality should be overlooked, He is carefully and at once declared to be God."

The teaching of Arius was rejected at the first ecumenical council at Nicea in Bithynia in A.D. 325, and the church's belief stated in the following terms (this is not the Nicene Creed: that was sanctioned at Chalcedon in A.D. 451):

> We believe in one God the Father almighty, Maker of all things visible and invisible; and in one Lord Jesus Christ, the Son of God, begotten of the Father, only-begotten, that is to say of the essence of the Father, God of God, Light of Light, true God of true God, begotten, not made, of the same essence as the Father; through whom all things were made, things in heaven and things on earth; who for us men and for our salvation, came down and became flesh and lived among men, who suffered and on the third day rose again, ascended into heaven, is coming to judge the living and the

dead; and in the Holy Spirit. But those who say, "There was a time when He was not," or "Before He was begotten He did not exist," and "He came into being from that which is nonexistent," or those who maintain that the Son of God is "of another substance or essence," or "created," or "capable of change," or "subject to alteration"—those the holy catholic and apostolic church pronounces accursed.

In the latter part of the century, Apollinaris, bishop of Laodicea, introduced the theory that our Lord possessed a human body and a human soul, but not a rational spirit. The place of rational spirit or mind was taken by the Logos. Apollinarianism, therefore, substituted a God clothed in flesh (*theos sarkophoros*) for a real God-man (*theanthropos*). As Athanasius pertinently asked, "How could Christ represent for us the pattern of the holy life after which we ought to strive, if His nature was not entirely homogeneous with ours? He could not redeem human nature in its completeness, unless He had Himself assumed all the parts of which it consists." Apollinarianism virtually denied a real incarnation, and this heretical teaching was condemned by the general council of Constantinople in A.D. 381, which maintained the traditional view that our Lord had two natures.

The attempt to explain the possession of two natures and only one personality led to further error, the Antiochian school distinguishing between the natures and viewing them as merely associated, while the Alexandrians insisted that the two were commingled and had coalesced. Nestorius, bishop of Constantinople, held that the Lord had two natures, divine and human, which were in some loose mechanical conjunction. Mary was the mother of the human but not of the divine. The Nestorian view divided the natures in such a way as to suggest that there were actually two personalities. Nestorianism was accordingly condemned at the council of Ephesus in A.D. 431, but the conflict continued to rage for another twenty years.

Eutyches, one of the presbyters of Constantinople, went farther than the bishop and declared that our Lord's two natures coalesced into one (from which originated the name Monophysitism), the human nature being absorbed into the divine. This doctrine was condemned at the Council of Chalcedon in A.D. 451, although Eutychianism itself did not come to an end as a result. At Chalcedon a fresh statement of the church's belief was issued in the following terms:

> Following the holy fathers, we with one consent teach men to confess one and the same Son, our Lord Jesus Christ, at once perfect in Godhead and also perfect in Manhood, truly God and truly Man, consisting of a rational soul and body; consubstantial with the Father in respect of His Godhead, and consubstantial with us in respect of His Manhood, like us in all respects, sin excepted. As regards His deity, begotten of the Father before all ages, but as regards His humanity in these last days born of the Virgin Mary, the mother of God, for us and for our salvation; one and the same Christ, Son, Lord, only-begotten, to be acknowledged in two natures, unmingled, immutable, indivisible, inseparable; the distinction of natures being by no means obliterated by their union but rather the property of each nature being preserved and being united in one Person and one subsistence, not divided or separated into two persons, but one and the same Son, and only-begotten, God the Word, the Lord Jesus Christ; as the prophets of old time have spoken concerning Him, and our Lord Jesus Christ taught us, and the belief of the fathers has delivered to us.

This statement has been described as a lighthouse to show the channel between the reefs of Nestorian Dyophysitism and Eutychian Monophysitism. It went farther, however, and, as Griffith Thomas has pointed out, it really dealt with Arianism which denied the true Godhead of Christ, with Apollinarianism which denied the perfect Manhood of Christ, with Nestorianism which denied the unity of the Person of Christ, and with Eutychianism which denied the distinction of the natures of Christ.

Chalcedon did not dispose of the matter, unfortunately.

The Monophysite controversy was long, violent, and acrimonious, and continued for two centuries. Eventually the Emperor Heraclius endeavored to reconcile the two parties by proposing as a basis of agreement that our Lord had two natures but only one will. This only gave rise to fresh conflict. Some accepted the imperial suggestion, but their view, Monotheletism, was condemned by the sixth general council at Constantinople in A.D. 681. The council decided "that in the one person of Christ, as there are two distinct natures, human and divine, there are of necessity two intelligences and two wills, the one fallible and finite, the other immutable and infinite." The Dyotheletic doctrine of two wills remains accepted to the present day, but it should be emphasized that our Lord's human will has always been considered to have been subordinate to His divine will.

Towards the end of the eighth century certain Spanish theologians, particularly Elipandus of Toledo and Felix of Urgellis, sought to find a solution to the problem of Dyophysitism. They contended that there were two modes of sonship in Christ, one natural and the other adoptive. As the son of Mary, He was the adopted Son of God: as the second Person in the Trinity, He was the only-begotten of the Father. In the first capacity He was subordinate to the Father, in the other He was an equal. This naturally did not find general acceptance, and adoptionism was condemned at Regensburg in A.D. 792, at Frankfort in A.D. 794 and at Aachen in A.D. 799.

Little further developed in Christological doctrine until the sixteenth century, when Martin Luther made a new (if doubtful) contribution. "Jesus Christ is true God," said Luther, "born of the Father in eternity, and also true man, born of the Virgin Mary." In teaching the inseparable union of the human and the divine natures in the Person of Christ, however, he propounded the theory that they interpenetrated one another in such a way that the attributes of the divine were communicated to the human. The incarnation, therefore, virtually deified the human nature (which was not divine *ex se*) in the womb of the Virgin Mary. During His earthly life our Lord veiled the divine perfections of His human nature, but these are now manifested in His exaltation. It was perhaps a natural corollary that the physical body was regarded as omnipresent and that Luther taught the real presence of Christ's body and blood in the elements of the Lord's Supper (i.e., consubstantiation as distinct from the Roman Catholic doctrine of transubstantiation).

Lutheranism was split by a later controversy between the divines of the two universities of Giessen and Tubingen. The former adopted a form of kenosis theory, taking the view that our Lord abstained from the use of His divine attributes during His humiliation; the latter followed the krypsis theory that He used them secretly. Yet little is left to be desired by the Augsburg Confession of A.D. 1553, "that the Word or Son of God was made a very Man," as amplified by the Würtemberg Confession ten years later to cover the fact of our Lord's eternal generation and consubstantiality in the words, "Begotten from everlasting of the Father, the very and eternal God, and of one substance with the Father."

During the same period the country of Poland produced a different kind of heresy in Socinianism. This derived from Faustus Socinus, an Italian freethinker, who denied the Trinity and insisted that "plurality of persons in one divine essence is impossible." He maintained that God was inscrutable, although He had revealed Himself in Christ, but that the latter was only a man with no existence prior to His human birth. Christ was miraculously conceived by the Virgin Mary; although peccable, He was sinless; He was baptized of the Holy Spirit to equip Him for His mission; and was caught up to Heaven to be taught by God before commencing His public ministry. At His exaltation, according to Socinus, universal authority and power became His, and He is now rightly worshiped as God. Socinians flourished in Poland until their expulsion in 1658, but their followers have now practically died out, although reflections of their teaching periodically appear in philosophical writings even today.

Of later developments it is perhaps worth mentioning the Presbyterian credal statement of the seventeenth century, commonly known as the Westminster Confession. This avers that:

> The Son of God, the second person in the Trinity, being very and eternal God, of one substance, and equal with the Father, did, when the fullness of time was come, take upon Him man's nature, and all the essential properties and common infirmities thereof, yet without sin: being conceived by the power of the Holy Ghost, in the womb of the Virgin Mary, of her substance. So that two whole, perfect, and distinct natures, the Godhead and the Manhood, were inseparably joined together in one person, without conversion, composition, or confusion. Which person is very God and very man, yet one Christ, the only Mediator between God and man.

It would be difficult to find fault with this clear and incisive statement.

In the first half of the following century the mystical philosophy of Swedenborgianism made some impression upon the thoughtful. Emmanuel Swedenborg taught that God always possessed a human form since He had a spiritual body as well as divine essence. At the incarnation He assumed a material body in addition to the spiritual one. This heretical teaching found a limited number of adherents but it is still not without its followers.

The eighteenth century was marked by the introduction of rationalism into the church. Immanuel Kant, of Königsberg, was the most outstanding of the rationalistic philosophers and the most active in propagating a purely humanistic view of Christ. Kant's thesis was that God was inscrutable: the historical Christ was an ideal and was set before the mind as the perfect man. He ceased to be an object of veneration when the mind had formed the ideal He represented. The true Christ was really the inward concept of a perfect man.

In many respects Kant prepared the way for the theologian Schleiermacher and his followers, who thought that God was unknowable. This school taught that Christ had no existence prior to Bethlehem, but that He was created as an ideal and sinlessly perfect man, His very sinlessness constituting His divinity. A God-consciousness controlled His whole life, so that He was in fact God manifest in flesh. His mission was to awaken the dormant God-consciousness in men, redemption being virtually effected by the liberation of that God-consciousness in the individual and his elevation thereby to the level of Christ, the ideal man. The utterances from some pulpits today show that this somewhat illogical heresy is not completely outmoded.

First propounded by Zinzendorf and subsequently developed more fully by German divines of the Lutheran confession, the modern kenotic theory established a firm grasp on many eminent theologians—and continues to do so. This theory is that, during His earthly life, our Lord completely abandoned His divine attributes and voluntarily restricted Himself to the natural limitations of man. In other words, He emptied Himself not only of His glory but also of His divine mode of existence (*morphe theou*) and assumed the human mode of existence as a servant (*morphe doulou*). The implication is not merely that the Logos assumed a human nature, which was itself subject to all the normal human limitations, but that the Logos was personally limited in this manner—i.e., as Schaff puts it, a "temporary self-exinanition or depotentiation of the preexistent Logos." This, of course, was a metaphysical impossibility: apart from anything else, it would virtually have involved a suspension of the intertrinitarian process for thirty-three years, and would have been in direct contradiction of the essential immutability of God. Gess and Ebrard went even farther in a suggestion that, at the incarnation, the Logos was actually transformed into a rational human soul, but this view found little support.

A later theory was that of a progressive impartation of the Logos to Christ. As the human nature developed and Christ's consciousness increased in capacity, so, it was argued, there was a further communication of the Logos up to the limits of our Lord's capacity at the time. This theory, too, has attracted very little support.

In the latter half of the nineteenth century, Albrecht Ritschl's lectures at Göttingen resulted in another school of thought. The Ritschlian view was that God has revealed Himself in Christ: indeed, it was an immanent necessity for God to reveal Himself to man. Christ was not preexistent, but He reflected all the attributes of deity, and His life had for man all the value of divinity. An ethical evaluation of Christ provided an estimate of His true (religious) worth.

The only contribution to Christological study during the twentieth century is the Barthian one, but precisely what Karl Barth understands is by no means clear. To some extent his theology is a blend of humanism and mysticism, but he declares that, by the incarnation, God took man's place, while man consequently took God's place—a somewhat fallacious and illogical proposition as stated, although it does, of course, contain a germ of truth.

The present century has also been marked by the rise of neoorthodoxy which, as expounded for example by Reinhold Niebuhr, has a distinctly Barthian emphasis. Neoorthodoxy, however, proves on examination to be little more than religious liberalism: its defenders will accept as truth only what is determinable by reason. There is no clear recognition of the deity of Christ, but the view regarding the incarnation resembles that of Karl Barth.

Griffith Thomas's comment in *The Principles of Theology* provides a suitable recapitulation of the development of

Christological doctrine. He says that there have been three main periods:

(1) Up to Chalcedon the church insisted on Christ as being very God and very Man. (2) From Chalcedon to 1900 the church approached, but did not solve, the union of natures. Before the Reformation the tendency was to lay too great stress on the divinity and to exclude the true view of His humanity. Since the Reformation the tendency has been to lay too great stress on the humanity and to exclude the true view of His divinity. (3) Since 1900, thinkers have been attempting to realize the unity of Christ's personal consciousness as seen in the New Testament, and to harmonize this with the clear distinction of natures, human and divine.

In the following pages James Gunn confines himself almost entirely to the scriptural teaching on the various facets of our Lord's life and work, and we commend this helpful and heart-warming book.

FREDK. A. TATFORD

1
THE ETERNAL CHRIST

The English name which we Christians give to the Supreme Being is God. This English word does not reveal anything regarding the divine essence as do the Hebrew names for God. It reveals rather the yearning of the human heart. The name God is derived from an English root that means to call; it implies that man in his extremity calls upon God, who is the Almighty. Not all men call upon Him: the atheist, the agnostic, and the careless do not usually call upon Him, but under adversity they may.

Parents generally give to their children names of which they are fond, or names of forebears, or perhaps names which suggest characteristics which they hope their children will develop. Unlike such names, the Hebrew appellations for God found in the Holy Scriptures reveal His nature and His attributes. Among the Hebrew names there are four which may be considered basic. They are prominent throughout the Old Testament: Elohim, Jehovah, El Shaddai, and Adonai.

Elohim is the first name for God in the Hebrew canon; it repeatedly occurs in Genesis chapter one: "In the beginning God created the heaven and the earth." It indicates that God is all powerful, that His might and wisdom are unlimited.

It is especially interesting that the name Elohim is a plural noun, and is used with singular verbs. In the Hebrew language there are singular nouns, which, of course, mean one. There are also dual nouns which mean two, and plural nouns which mean three or more. That God is pictured in the plural intimates that He is triunity—the Holy Trinity.

Jehovah is the next name for God in the Bible chronologically. The name Jehovah in the King James Version is printed in all capital letters, LORD. The Spirit of God, through whom the Scriptures were indited, frequently uses the name Jehovah in Genesis 2—3. It has been estimated that this name occurs more than six thousand five hundred times in the Hebrew of the Old Testament. To certain Jewish persons this name is so awesome that, when reading the Word of God, they do not pronounce it. Occasionally they will substitute and use Adonai, or just pause.

The name Jehovah is derived from the Hebrew verb "to be." God's own definition is found in Exodus 3. In speaking to Moses, God describes His very essence in the Words, "I AM THAT I AM." A modern exposition is, "I will be that I will be." Here is One who is absolutely immutable and eternal. There is involved in this appellation the facts that God is the Eternally-Existent, the Ever-Existent, and the Self-Existent One. All this is seen in the miracle of the burning bush (Exodus 3:2-5). As the flame continued without fuel, God is self-sustained. As the bush was wrapped about by flames but remained unconsumed, so God is unchangeable. From within the burning bush a human voice spoke to Moses. We need not be surprised to read, "Moses was afraid to look upon God."

The third name is El Shaddai. *El* is an abbreviated form of Elohim and consequently means Mighty One. The Hebrew word *shad* is translated in the King James Version as breast, usually used of a woman's breast. Some have suggested that in the name El Shaddai there is intimated a feminine picture of God but this is difficult to accept for all the other titles are in the masculine. The idea is the all-sufficiency of God. As a mother nourishes, loves, and sustains her child from within herself, so God is abundantly able to comfort and satisfy His own. His resources are inexhaustible. Perhaps among the many apocalyptic pictures of Christ in the book of the Revelation there is a suggested portrait of El Shaddai: "And in the midst of the seven candlesticks one like unto the Son of man, clothed with a garment down to the foot, and girt about the breast with a golden girdle" (Revelation 1:13).

This precious name occurs for the first time in Genesis 17:1-2, where it is rendered, "I am the Almighty God." Abraham here is promised that eventually he will have a son. God is perfectly able to meet the need of Abraham and his wife Sarah. It is the divine intention that in Abraham's son all nations of the earth be blessed.

The name Adonai is equivalent to husband or master, therefore implying both relationship and authority. There is an excellent illustration of its use in Isaiah 6:1-8. When Isaiah saw the Lord (Adonai) high and lifted up, and His train filling the temple, he cried, "Woe is me! for . . . I am a man of unclean lips, and I dwell in the midst of a people of unclean lips: for mine eyes have seen the King, the LORD [Jehovah] of hosts. Also I heard the voice of the Lord [Adonai], saying Whom shall I send, and who will go for Us? Then said I, Here am I; send me." He heard the voice of divine authority, his Master's voice.

Such then is the God before whom men bow in adoring worship, the God whom we may call upon in the hour of distress and need. Frequently we have overheard the heart cry, "Oh, God! Oh, God!"—the plaintive appeal which accompanies groanings which cannot be uttered (Romans 8:26).

The Holy Trinity

Reference has already been made to a plurality in God. This plurality is called the Trinity. The divine Trinity is composed of Father, Son, and Holy Spirit. Although we thus speak of God, we must ever remember that He is one: "Hear,

O Israel: The LORD our God is one LORD [Jehovah]'' (Deuteronomy 6:4). ''There is one God, and one mediator between God and men, the man Christ Jesus'' (1 Timothy 2:5). Monotheism (belief in one only God) has been the testimony of Judaism throughout the centuries. Mohammedanism also maintains a belief in only one God. In spite of the criticism of Judaism, monotheism is the testimony of the Christian Church. She believes in the threefold distinctions, Father, Son, and Holy Spirit, who are one in essence, one in power, one in wisdom. The Lord our God is one Lord.

There are numerous occasions in both the Old and New Testaments when the oneness and the triunity of the Godhead are evident; for example, ''God said, Let Us make man in Our image, after Our likeness'' (Genesis 1:26). ''And the LORD God said, Behold, the man is become as one of Us'' (Genesis 3:22). Isaiah records God as saying, ''Whom shall I send, and who will go for Us?'' (Isaiah 6:8)

Of course, in the New Testament the Holy Trinity is obvious. At the baptism of our Lord Jesus, ''The heavens were opened unto Him, and He saw the Spirit of God descending like a dove, and lighting upon Him: and lo a voice from heaven, saying, This is My beloved Son, in whom I am well pleased'' (Matthew 3:16-17). The Trinity is also evident in the apostolic benediction: ''The grace of the Lord Jesus Christ, and the love of God, and the communion of the Holy Spirit, be with you all. Amen'' (2 Corinthians 13:14).

Thomas Newberry, editor of ''the Englishman's Bible,'' uses solar light as an illustration of the divine Trinity. He suggests that, since the Eternal God dwells in light which no man can approach (1 Timothy 6:16), light must therefore be eternal:

> Light is a formation and arrangement of infinite skill, wisdom, and goodness. As no ray of white light has ever proceeded from the sun which by the prism could not be divided into its three elemen-

tary colors: yellow, red, and blue, so every revelation that God has made of Himself has been ever of the Father, Son, and Spirit in the one undivided Deity.[1]

Eternal Counsels

Most, at one time or another, have heard the expression, "The eternal counsels of God." The very idea stimulates interest. At any counsel, prudence and wisdom are in evidence in the mutual exchange of thought and deliberation, and important decisions are made.

Perhaps even a limited apprehension of what transpired within the Godhead will enable us to appreciate the historical fact that the Father sent the Son to be the Saviour of the world (1 John 4:14).

The governors and princes which accused Daniel spoke of the "laws of the Medes and Persians which altereth not" (Daniel 6:12). The law of the Medes and Persians have not only been changed, but that great empire has been completely vanquished and is no more. In contrast we read, "The counsel of the LORD standeth for ever, the thoughts of His heart to all generations" (Psalm 33:11). His oath and His promises are alike immutable (Hebrews 6:17).

There are several intimations of these divine eternal counsels in the Bible. The Lord Jesus was foreordained (He was set forth or displayed) before the foundation of the world to be the sacrifice which was to accomplish redemption. He was manifested in time for us (1 Peter 1:19-20). The clause, "Who . . . was manifested in these times for you," probably means that the Saviour was made visible (there is a subtle hint here of the incarnation of the Lord Jesus) at the end of certain specific periods which are sometimes called dispensations. The last of these in Peter's day was the period of grace in which he lived, the period in which we all live now.

---

[1]Thomas Newberry, *Solar Light as Illustrating Trinity in Unity,* page 11.

There have been a number of distinctive periods in human history; for example, a period of innocence in Eden, a period of conscience—a conscience stifled by Cain, a period of promises made to Abraham and to his descendants, etc.

The Apostle Paul introduced the Ephesians to some of the eternal counsels concerning the people of God: "Blessed be the God and Father of our Lord Jesus Christ, who hath blessed us with all spiritual blessings in heavenly places in Christ: according as He hath chosen us in Him before the foundation of the world" (Ephesians 1:3-4). In that indefinite past God spoke well of us, for such is the meaning of the verb "bless" that is used here; consequently we should bless Him, speak well of Him, praise Him. Ours indeed should be an attitude of adoration and thanksgiving.

All this arises from the fact that the Lord chose us for Himself in that premundane act when He blessed us. The verbs "to bless" and "to choose" are both in the same tense. The final issue of being thus blessed and chosen will be the joy and the love of the Father's immediate presence. Here we bow in adoration and worship. Our hearts are humbled that the Lord should ever have looked upon us in mercy, so ill-deserving are we. He who is perfect in righteousness and love has selected us as His very own possession.

In the perfections which we have now in Christ, and which eventually shall be experienced, the Lord will show to all universal intelligence the exceeding riches of His grace (Ephesians 2:7). O the depth of the riches both of the wisdom and knowledge of God! Let His name be extolled and acclaimed.

Election—God's choice of us—is according to the sovereign will of God; it is therefore futile to evade the difficulties which this doctrine presents. Man is ruined by sin: "As by one man sin entered into the world, and death by sin; so that death has passed upon all men for all have sinned" (Romans 5:12). Indubitably death upon mankind was in all its aspects: spiritual, physical, and eternal. Yet, in spite of such a penalty—a just penalty—God in grace and goodness has chosen certain ones.

It is regrettable that some have the idea that God chose only the Church as a body, and that an individual is not among the elect until he exercises faith in Christ and thus places himself in that body. To assert that election is not to salvation but to service and testimony is to ignore some of the plain statements of Holy Scripture. Election is of the individual and for each elect person He has an eternal purpose: "According as He hath chosen us in Him before the foundation of the world, that we should be holy and without blame before Him in love" (Ephesians 1:4). What a prospect! Then shall we be perfect but not until then. The believer's standing in Christ is so complete (Colossians 2:10) that he is assured of the most intimate and perfect position in the immediate precincts of God.

In praying for the members of His Church who would believe through apostolic ministry, the Lord Jesus requested, "Father, I will that they also, whom Thou hast given Me, be with Me where I am; that they may behold My glory, which Thou hast given Me . . . before the foundation of the world" (John 17:24). Rufus was chosen as an individual (Romans 16:13). The Apostle John uses this concept in a very personal manner: "The elect lady" (2 John 1), "The children of thy elect sister greet thee" (2 John 13). There is no authority within this Epistle to spiritualize these figures. We must therefore accept them literally.

Peter's understanding of election certainly has the individual in view, and definitely unto salvation through the work of the Holy Spirit and the redemptive work of Christ: "Elect according to the foreknowledge of God the Father, through sanctification of the Spirit, unto obedience and sprinkling of the blood of Jesus Christ" (1 Peter 1:2).

John Murray writes in *Baker's Dictionary of Theology*:

> As election is eternal so is it sovereign. No passage shows this more clearly than Romans 9:11, where the differentiation between Esau and Jacob finds its explanation in, and is directed to the vindication of "the purpose of God according to election." It is futile to appeal to the foreknowledge of God as in any way abridging or modifying the sovereign character of election. Romans 8:29 shows that the tern "foreknow" is itself differentiating and cannot mean the foresight of faith but refers to that distinguishing knowledge of God by which He loved the persons concerned from Eternity. Romans 8:29 is similar to Ephesians 1:5, that in love God predestinated His people unto adoption. Foreknowledge is the synonym of "forelove" and so whom He "foreknew" (Romans 8:29) is equivalent to election in Christ (Ephesians 1:4).

There is another glimpse of the consultations within the Godhead which directs our attention to the Lord Jesus and to His accomplished work at Calvary. It is found in Peter's pentecostal address. This once cowardly apostle, now full of the Holy Spirit, is the spokesman for all the others during a remarkable occasion: "Ye men of Israel, hear these words; Jesus of Nazareth, a man approved of God among you by miracles and wonders and signs, which God did by Him in the midst of you, as ye yourselves know: Him, being delivered by the determinate counsel and foreknowledge of God, ye have taken, and by wicked hands have crucified and slain: Whom God hath raised up, having loosed the pains of death: because it was not possible that He should be holden of it" (Acts 2:22-24).

Thomas Walker of India in his commentary, *The Book of the Acts,* asserts: "He [the Father] deliberately handed over the Son of His love into the hands of His enemies for the redemption of the world."[1] He also notes that the word "determinate" means to appoint, to determine, and to

[1]Thomas Walker, *The Book of the Acts,* page 45.

decree, and then continues, "God's plan and purpose in the atonement were formulated and determined on before the world began" (Revelation 13:8; 2 Timothy 1:9). These divine plans and purposes indicate that the Lord Jesus is eternal.

As in the mystery of the incarnation, even so in the reconciliatory work of our Saviour there are depths which we cannot plumb. It is evident that the death of the Lord Jesus was neither an emergency nor an accident. It was carefully devised and executed.

The Eternal Christ

Do we just assume that the Lord Jesus Christ was eternal or do the Holy Scriptures present Him as such? The latter certainly is true. Isaiah wrote of the Messiah, "Unto us a child is born [the humanity of Christ], unto us a son is given [the deity of Christ]: and the government shall be upon His shoulder: and His name shall be called Wonderful, Counsellor, The mighty God, The everlasting Father, The Prince of Peace" (Isaiah 9:6).

What a revelation of His attributes! "The Everlasting Father" is variously translated. In the Vulgate it is rendered, "The Father of the future age." Elsewhere it is given the meaning, "The Father of the Everlasting Age" and "The Father of Eternity." Obviously the Son of God is here pictured as the paternal source of Eternity. How forceful is this descriptive appellation! If it were possible to conceive the origin of Eternity, the Lord Jesus is that origin.

Micah makes a very important prediction, "But thou, Bethlehem Ephratah, though thou be little among the thousands of Judah, yet out of thee shall He come forth unto Me that is to be ruler in Israel; whose goings forth have been from of old, from everlasting, from the days of Eternity" (Micah 5:2 NASV).

Dr. Fredk. A. Tatford says in his little volume, *The Prophet of Messiah's Advent*:

> No new personality came into existence at Bethlehem when Jesus was born. The Eternal had become incarnate. God had taken manhood unto Himself and the child of Mary was—and always will be—the God Man. What He had ever been in the ages of the past, He continued to be in incarnation.[1]

There are several somewhat similar assertions in the New Testament: "In the beginning was the Word, and the Word was with God, and the Word was God" (John 1:1). The question naturally arises, to what does John make reference by "the beginning"? Is it the beginning of creation? Is it the beginning of Christ's life here on earth, His incarnation? Or is it perhaps that the word is used in a very abstract way, John implying that whenever the beginning was, the Word preexisted it and was already manifest? Here then we have the preexistence of an individual. That point is quite clear.

"And the Word was with God." This preexistent One was "with" God. The preposition "with" suggests association. "The same was in the beginning with God." Furthermore it is also stated, "And the Word was [continuously] God." What dogmatism! What a declaration of Deity! How shall we then regard the Word? Indubitably this preexistent individual, who associated with God and who bears the descriptive title "the Word," is Deity Himself, God manifest in flesh. "The Word was made flesh, and dwelt among us, (and we beheld His glory, the glory as of the only begotten of the Father,) full of grace and truth" (John 1:14). The word "dwell" (tabernacle) suggests the sanctuary in the wilderness with the pillar cloud of glory arising from its rear room. There was such a glory cloud about the Saviour when He was here, figuratively speaking.

It is said that the ancient Chinese divided their words into two general categories, dead words and living words. Nouns, adjectives, adverbs, prepositions, etc., were dead words. You might have a long list of words that do not make a statement. Verbs are living words, words of action; they speak and fit into the second category. Here then John introduces us to the Living Word, the Living Word which speaks: "No man hath seen God at any time; the only begotten Son [a number of very good manuscripts read, "only begotten God"], which is in the bosom of the Father, He hath declared Him" (John 1:18).

In the Spanish translation of John's Gospel (1569 A.D. version, the most recent revision 1960) verse one reads, *En el principio era el Verbo,* "In the beginning was the Verb." In Christ we have therefore the full expression of the Father's love, power, and purpose.

John also records for us some of the claims of the Lord Jesus; for example, "Before Abraham was I am." Some of the more modern translations read, "Before Abraham was born, I am," but that does not change the meaning. The contrast between Abraham and Jesus is a contrast between one whose existence had a beginning and One who always existed, One without a beginning and without an end. This blessed One has a continuous, present existence.

The Jews understood immediately the claims of Christ, just as they did when the Lord Jesus spoke the parable of the Good Shepherd and said, "I and My Father are one. Then took they up stones to cast at Him." To this they added, "For a good work we stone Thee not; but for blasphemy; and because that Thou, being a man, makest Thyself God" (John 10:30-33).

In the fourth century of the Christian era there arose a heresy named Arianism. Arius, the propagator of this error, overemphasized the word "begotten" with reference to our

---

[1]Fredk. A. Tatford, *The Prophet of Messiah's Advent,* page 67.

Lord's being the only begotten Son. Arius contended that if the Father begat the Son, then the Son had a beginning of existence, and was therefore inferior to the Father. This heresy was refuted and Arius was expelled from the church at the Council of Nicea, A.D. 325.

Part of the doctrine of the so-called Jehovah's Witnesses is merely a revival of the Arianism of the fourth century. This modern cult has placed an unholy import upon the words of the Apostle Paul, "The firstborn of every creature" (Colossians 1:15-19). They contend that the Father created the Son, that the Son might create all else. In so doing they deny the eternal existence of the Lord Jesus Christ. In so doing they ignore the remainder of this great Christological passage: "By Him were all things created, that are in heaven, and that are in earth, visible and invisible, whether they be thrones, or dominions, or principalities, or powers: all things were created by Him and for Him. And He is before all things, and by Him all things consist." He is not one of the created elements, He predates them all. Furthermore, "It pleased the Father that in Him should all fullness dwell." In chapter two there is a related statement which is more explicit, "In Him dwelleth all the fullness of the Godhead bodily" (Colossians 2:9).

The perversion of this same cult relative to the meaning in Scripture of the appellation "firstborn" is very subtle. That the title "firstborn" may be used literally of the first of a woman's offspring there is no doubt. The final plague to fall upon the Egyptians at the time of Israel's deliverance from their slavery was the death of all the firstborn. The Lord had declared, "All the firstborn in the land of Egypt shall die, from the firstborn of Pharaoh that sitteth upon his throne, even unto the firstborn of the maidservant that is behind the mill; and all the firstborn of beasts" (Exodus 11:5).

Notwithstanding, the title is also used figuratively in the

Word of God. Its use implies a superlative, something of the greatest possible degree. The Lord uses it to describe Israel: "Thus saith the LORD, Israel is My son, even My firstborn" (Exodus 4:22). This cannot mean that Israel was the first original nation. There were nations and even empires before she came into existence. Israel as the firstborn was the nearest people to God's heart. His thoughts of Israel were tender and benevolent. That nation had the preeminent place in God's thoughts. This is evident in the divine affirmation: "I will make him My firstborn, higher than the kings of the earth" (Psalm 89:27). None would be greater than Israel.

Bildad, as he answers some of Job's remarks, speaks of a destructive disease which he calls the "firstborn of death." He distinguishes this fatal illness as worse than all others, as if it were the culmination of all deaths.

Isaiah also uses the term firstborn in a figurative sense: "The firstborn of the poor shall feed, and the needy shall lie down in safety" (Isaiah 14:30). The prediction was to the effect that after the enemy had been destroyed, the poorest of the poor would be well fed.

It is surely not difficult to see that in the figurative use of the word, firstborn, Christ is superlatively greater than all; He transcends everyone. He is "the firstborn of all creation" (Colossians 1:15-17) because He is far above and beyond creation. "He is before all things," and is supreme over them.

The Lord Jesus is in like manner "the firstborn from the dead" (Colossians 1:18; Revelation 1:5). "Now is Christ risen from the dead, and become the firstfruits of them that slept" (1 Corinthians 15:20). Both "firstfruits" and "firstborn" are used synonymously. "That in all things He might have the preeminence" (Colossians 1:18). In resurrection as in all else, Christ has the priority.

How wonderful the divine family must be! "For whom He [God the Father] did foreknow, He also did predestinate to be conformed to the image of His Son, that He might be the firstborn among many brethren'' (Romans 8:29).

Under the law the firstborn received the inheritance and the special patriarchal blessing. Esau, Isaac's firstborn, despised these and sold them for a mess of pottage (Genesis 25:29-34). The firstborn had authority over his brethren. He also received a double portion, as well as a place in the early priesthood. What a foreshadowing of the perfect Firstborn! All believers are destined to bear the image of God's Son that He might be supreme and transcendent among many brethren.

Man was created in the image of God, but that image was marred in the fall through sin. We read that Adam ''begat a son in his own likeness, after his image'' (Genesis 5:3). Through the redemptive work of Christ, God is restoring the divine image to all believers (Romans 8:29). All in that family will resemble the Lord Jesus.

The writer to the Hebrews identifies members of the Church as the ''firstborn.'' He says that we have come ''to the general assembly and church of the firstborn, which are written in heaven'' (Hebrews 12:23). The meaning here apparently is that the members of the Church universal are honored in splendor and glory. Grace has distinguished them and has given them a first place in the purposes of God.

2
THE VIRGIN BIRTH

Inasmuch as the virgin birth of Christ is considered by many to be a biological impossibility and consequently a natural improbability, is it an essential part of sound Christian doctrine? It is denied and derided by disbelievers and heretics, questioned even by many churchmen, and thought of as a myth or farce by some professing Christians. The question occasionally is asked, is it necessary to believe in the doctrine of the virgin birth to be saved? This may be emphatically asserted: the virgin birth of Christ is an integral part of the plan of salvation; without it as an actual historical fact there could be no redemption for ruined man.

There are those who claim to have found the source of this story in the imagination of early Jewish Christians. As the gospel was disseminated throughout the Roman world, Christ was its theme, and of course He was the center of the resulting community of believers. Therefore to make this great spiritual and social leader even more spectacular the story of the virgin birth was conceived and propagated. This foolish and offensive idea ignores completely the narratives of our Saviour's birth as recorded by both Matthew and Luke. It is not only a repudiation of this basic doctrine but it is a denial of the inerrant, inspired Word of God.

The Necessity of the Virgin Birth

The processes of natural generation result in a man being born, born in sin and shapen in iniquity (Psalm 51:5). The

Word of God declares, "As by one man sin entered into the world, and death by sin; and so death passed upon all men, for that all have sinned" (Romans 5:12). This of course means that all are seen by God to have sinned and died in the federal head of the human race, Adam. With the transmission of life there has been the transmission of sin and death. Job has poetically yet realistically described humanity: "Man that is born of a woman is of few days, and full of trouble. He cometh forth like a flower, and is cut down: he fleeth also as a shadow, and continueth not. . . . Who can bring a clean thing out of an unclean? not one" (Job 14:1-4).

In contrast to all this we read, "When the fullness of time was come, God sent forth His Son, made of a woman, made under the law" (Galatians 4:4). This holy and eternal Son of God was without blemish and without spot (1 Peter 1:19), perfectly sinless and pure. Would it therefore be reasonable that God send His Son, "that Holy Thing," the Light of Lights, the only impeccable man, into the world by the same process of natural generation? It would not! God in sending His Son chose an altogether different means, that of miraculous generation. That is to say, the conception of our Lord by Mary was miraculous, it was by the Holy Spirit, but His birth was natural. The virgin birth was the single method selected by God for the coming of Christ into the world.

The doctrine of the virgin birth is likewise very, very important to an understanding of the faultless, stainless nature of the Lord Jesus Christ. The Apostle Paul describes the evil nature with which man, as a descendant of Adam is born: "I am carnal, sold under sin. . . . I know that in me (that is, in my flesh,) dwelleth no good thing. . . . When I would do good, evil is present with me. . . . O wretched man that I am! who shall deliver me from the body of this death?" (Romans 7:14-25) It is fundamentally true that man is not a sinner because he sins, but rather that he sins because he is a sinner. This is his nature, the effect of the fall.

Our blessed Lord Jesus did not inherit a sinful nature. He was made in the likeness of sinful flesh (Romans 8:3), but not in sinful flesh. He was "that holy thing" that was to be born (Luke 1:35), "the Seed of the woman" (Genesis 3:15). Consequently, the very nature of the Lord was purity itself. In regard to His temptation, this should be said: "The whole matter is, not that He did not sin, but rather that He could not sin." On one occasion the Lord said, "The prince of this world cometh, and hath nothing in Me" (John 14:30). Satan could find no sin in Christ, therefore there was nothing by which he could lay hold of the Lord Jesus. Because of His sinlessness Christ was ever beyond the reach and hold of the devil. Furthermore, the writer of the Epistle to the Hebrews writes by inspiration: "We have not an high priest which cannot be touched with the feeling of our infirmities; but was in all points tempted like as we are, yet without sin" (Hebrews 4:14). Christ was separate, apart from sin. Sin was no temptation to the Lord.

The practice of the ceremonial law in Israel taught that nation, and through that nation, us: first, that "the soul that sinneth, it shall die" (Ezekiel 18:4), and that the penalty of sin is death: "the wages of sin is death" (Romans 6:23).

In the second place, the same law of the offerings indicates that the penalty of sin, death, may be suffered by a substitute, but that such a substitute must be perfect. Each animal for sacrifice was carefully examined, it was searched for any defect whatever. The Lord Jesus is the substitute for each believer. Each one may say truthfully, "The life which I now live in the flesh I live by the faith of the Son of God, who loved me, and gave Himself for me" (Galatians 2:20). Physically we live "in the flesh"; spiritually we live "in the faith" (objective faith) of the Son of God who loved us. The proof of that love is that He became a substitute for every believer.

Not only do we learn that the penalty of sin may be endured vicariously, but that the substitute that was chosen had to be absolutely perfect. Any physical imperfection in the sacrificial victim resulted in its rejection. Any physical, mental, spiritual, or emotional deficiency in Christ would have disqualified His sacrifice when He offered Himself a sweet-smelling savor unto God for us (Ephesians 5:2).

The Word of God declares: "None of them can by any means redeem his brother, nor give to God a ransom for him" (Psalm 49:7). Jeremiah assures us that "every one shall die for his own iniquity" (Jeremiah 31:30). In order to save man, an absolutely sinless and immaculate substitute had to be provided. Christ is that substitute, and this is evident in the virgin birth. He is blameless before men; that is, without any disgrace in His public life. He is also without blemish before God, He is without an inward stain. Again it must be insisted, Christ was born "the Seed of the woman" through the power and influence of the eternal Spirit; He did not partake of Adam's depraved nature.

The virgin birth of Christ is an important event in the history of the incarnation. It alone explains the impeccability of our holy Lord; and through the virgin birth God provided a suitable, perfect substitute to suffer the penalty of human guilt and to secure salvation for all who believe in Him.

The Credibility of the Virgin Birth

There are many today, as there have been throughout the centuries, who discredit miracles. They logically reason from the standpoint that a virgin birth is a biological impossibility; they question the statement of our Lord, "With God all things are possible" (Matthew 19:26). Notwithstanding modern thought, during the ages of antiquity man believed that a virgin birth was possible and that it was to be expected.

Antiquity expected a virgin birth: God set the sun, moon, and stars in the heavens "for seasons, and for days, and years.'' Furthermore, He set the starry hosts in the heavens ''for signs'' (Genesis 1:14). From time immemorial signs and figures have been attached to the different constellations of fixed stars. There are twelve primary signs, and these twelve are called the zodiac. The encyclopedia says that the zodiac is of great antiquity, and that the region it occupies in the heavens was noted by different people independently. It contains all the known planets as well as the sun, moon, and many stars.

The first allusion to the zodiac is found in Genesis 11:4. In spite of the wrong italics in this text, the idea in the mind of the builders of Babel was to place the signs of the zodiac at the top of their tower (their ziggurat). Like so much that has been given to man, the zodiac was soon perverted and was used for idolatrous purposes.

Dr. Seiss in his volume, *The Gospel in the Stars,* quotes the following from a Professor Mitchell:

> We delight to honor the names of Kepler, Galileo, and Newton, but we must go beyond the epoch of the Deluge, and see our first discoveries among those sages whom God permitted to count their age by centuries, and there learn the order in which the secrets of the starry world yielded themselves up.[1]

There is every evidence, so we are told by scholars, that the signs of the zodiac were known long before the days of Noah, and were originally accepted as a divine symbolic revelation of the unfolding of God's plan of salvation for mankind. It is believed by many that these signs of the zodiac, this very early revelation, was added by the Lord to complement the witness of creation to her Creator.

The first of the twelve signs of the zodiac is Virgo, the virgin. In one hand she holds a sheaf of wheat for seed and in the other hand, she holds a branch. Christ is called in Scrip-

---

[1]Joseph A. Seiss, *The Gospel in the Stars,* page 59.

ture both the Seed of the woman and the Branch (Genesis 3:15; Zechariah 6:12).

Furthermore, close to the sign of Virgo is the sign of Coma. This is a picture of the same virgin holding in her arms the infant called Coma, meaning the Desired One, the Longed for One. Perhaps Haggai has this blessed One in mind when he speaks of "the desire of all nations" (Haggai 2:7). In some of the ancient languages, we are informed, the Hebrew name given to this child Coma is equivalent to the Greek name Christ.

Much more might be added to this section of our study of Virgo and Coma, but this will suffice to prove the suggestion that many of the ancients expected that eventually a virgin would bear a son.

Man in his sad and constant decline from God and His revelation became a polytheist, an idolater. A hundred years before Christ was born, because of what the pagans of Gaul saw in the zodiac, they had an altar upon which they placed this inscription, "To the virgin who is to bring forth." We deplore the idolatry of heathenism, nevertheless we are impressed by the latent belief in an eventual virgin birth.

The early Church believed in the virgin birth. The literature that has survived since the early centuries of the Christian era proves that there was implicit faith among the primitive Christians in the virgin birth of Christ. Here are some quotations from some of the fathers of the Christian Church.

Ignatius: an elder in the church at Antioch (Acts 13:1-3) who was martyred in A.D. 115 was ". . . fully persuaded as touching that He is truly of the race of David according to the flesh, but Son of God by the divine will and power, truly born of a virgin and baptized by John that all righteousness might be fulfilled by Him."

---

[1]J. Gresham Machen, *The Virgin Birth of Christ,* page 6 footnote.

Irenaeus who died at the close of the second century of the Christian era wrote:

> As Adam was first made from untilled soil and received his being from virgin earth, and was fashioned by the hand of God . . . so He who existed as the Word restored in Himself Adam, by His birth from Mary who was still a virgin, a birth befitting this restoration of Adam.[1]

Athanasius who lived in Alexandria during the close of the third and the beginning of the fourth centuries of this dispensation has left in his writings a very remarkable statement regarding the incarnation and virgin birth of our Lord:

> Aaron was not born a high-priest, but a man, and in course of time, when God willed, he became a high-priest . . . putting on over his usual clothes the ephod, breastplate, and robe . . . and thus clad he entered into the holy place and offered the sacrifice for the people. . . . So the Lord "In the beginning was the Word . . ." but when the Father willed that as Aaron put on his robe, so the Word took earthly flesh, having Mary for the mother of His body, to correspond to the virgin soil (from which Adam was made), that as a high-priest, Himself having as offering, He might offer Himself to the Father and cleanse us all from sins. . . . As Aaron remained the same and did not change by assuming the high-priest's dress . . . so the Lord did not become another by taking the flesh, but remained the same and was clothed in it.[2]

Logic confirms faith in the virgin birth. As we have already discovered from the Word of God, all men since Adam have been born by natural generation; consequently all have inherited Adam's fallen nature: "As through one man sin entered into the world, and death through sin, and so death spread to all men, because all sinned" (Romans 5:12 NASV). It just could not be otherwise. All beings who, during their existence live in sin, are born by the same natural biological process. This, of course, is not true of celestial beings,

---

[1]Henry Bettenson, *The Early Christian Fathers,* page 387

[2]Ibid.

seraphim, cherubim, and angels. Since it pleased God to send His own Son into the world, a Son who is eternal in His existence and infinitely pure and holy in His nature, it is expected that God would employ another distinct and separate process in the incarnation of that Son. This is surely what He has done. Ordinary men are born by natural generation; the Son of God, as has been demonstrated, was born into human life by means of miraculous generation.

The Denial of the Virgin Birth

The ministry of the Apostle Paul repeatedly was contradicted by Jewish professing Christians who mixed law with grace. They believed in the gospel, but they taught that it was also necessary to practice the law continuously and be circumcised. The apostle constantly had to refute their stand and their teaching.

J. Gresham Machen in his book, *The Virgin Birth of Christ,* has traced the development of the Jewish-Christian cult in the postapostolic years. Apparently it became divided into two heretical parties, the Nazarines and the Ebionites. There were serious doctrinal differences between these two parties.

The Nazarines accepted the gospel of Christ and its message of salvation; they were more orthodox than the others, and approved the ministry of Paul. They also recognized the liberty of the Gentiles from the law and from circumcision, but they themselves being Jews adhered to both of these practices. The Nazarines, as they were called, believed in the virgin birth of Christ.

The Ebionites not only practiced the law themselves but sought to force it upon the Gentiles. They discredited Paul's doctrine of free grace. Furthermore, they denied the virgin birth of our Lord. They seemed to be not only the successors of the Judaizers who harassed the Apostle Paul, but the followers of the apostates denounced in the Epistle to the Hebrews, the first Epistle of John, and the Epistle of Jude.

The doctrine of the Ebionites was probably not the first denial of the virgin birth of Christ, but it probably was the most concerted in the early centuries. It is obvious therefore that any denial of the virgin birth of Christ is not a modern departure from Biblical truth; it is merely the continuance or the survival of the ancient heresy of the Ebionites. A brief list of some who today deny the virgin birth could contain the following: Jews, Muhammadans, liberal Protestant theologians, Theosophists, Spiritualists, members of the Unity School of Christianity, etc. Although Christian Science, Jehovah's Witnesses, and the Seventh Day Adventists are heretical in numerous points of doctrine, these cults do accept in certain phases the virgin birth of Jesus. The first two are very heretical.

The Scriptures and the Virgin Birth

Before it is possible to formulate a doctrine of the virgin birth of Christ, it is necessary to examine what the Scriptures have to say on this subject.

The Old Testament: (1) Along with the curse upon the serpent, God prophesied Satan's final defeat: "I will put enmity between thee and the woman, and between thy seed and her seed; it shall bruise thy head, and thou shalt bruise His heel" (Genesis 3:15). While this statement cannot be considered a direct prediction of the virgin birth, it is nevertheless implied. It should be noticed that "the Seed of the woman" is singular, and in some translations is followed by the singular pronoun "He": "He shall bruise thy head." There is no doubt that this promised victory over Satan will be accomplished through the Lord Jesus who came "made of a woman, made under the law" (Galatians 4:4), albeit made miraculously.

Naturally the passage might have read (wrongly read, of course), "the seed of Adam," for he was the head of the human race. The fact that the promise was made in regard to the "Seed of the woman" indicates that He who was to come and finally to triumph over Satan would be no ordinary member of the human race.

That the appellation "the Seed of the woman" is primarily true of the Lord Jesus is clear from Paul's remarks to the Galatians: "The Scripture does not say 'and to seeds,' meaning many people but 'and to your seed,' meaning one person, who is Christ" (Galatians 3:16, NIV). Notwithstanding here we may have a double interpretation. As the seed of the serpent may embrace a plurality; even so, may the "Seed of the woman"; and may have a more extended application involving not only the Christ of God Himself but all those who are viewed as being in Him.

This then is the promise of triumph over evil as personified in Satan. It is the final victory of full redemption in the Lord Jesus.

(2) "The Lord Himself shall give you a sign; behold, a virgin shall conceive, and shall bear a son, and shall call His name Immanuel" (Isaiah 7:14). God had offered unbelieving Ahaz, king of Judah, a sign regarding the defeat of the allied enemies, Syria and Ephraim, but this foolish and incredulous man rejected the offer. However, God imposed upon him a sign, the sign of the Son of a virgin.

This prediction must be understood according to a principle of prophetical interpretation called the near and the distant fulfillment, or the partial and the complete fulfillment. The near, the partial fulfillment of God's sign to Ahaz is recorded in Isaiah 8:3-4: "I went unto the prophetess; and she conceived, and bare a son. Then said the Lord to me, call his name Maher-shalal-hash-baz. For before the child shall have knowledge to cry, my father, and my mother, the riches of Damascus and the spoil of Samaria shall be taken away before the king of Assyria.'' The son of the prophetess was a sign unto Ahaz, but he does not comply fully with the details of the prediction of Isaiah 7:14, for his name was not Immanuel; he had a father and a mother; his mother definitely was not a virgin. It is therefore necessary to seek the complete fulfillment in divine prophecy. This fulfillment is found in Matthew 1:22-23: Jesus who saves His people from their sins is Emmanuel, ''God with us.''

Isaiah provides an excellent example of partial immediate fulfillment and complete future fulfillment. There is the prophecy, ''Behold, a virgin [*almah,* a young marriageable woman who is still unmarried] shall conceive, and bear a son, and shall call His name Immanuel'' (7:14). There is the partial fulfillment in the son of the prophetess (8:1-4). The complete fulfillment is given in 9:6-7. In anticipation of the birth of Christ it is written, ''Unto us a child is born, unto us a Son is given: and the government shall be upon His shoulder: and His name shall be called Wonderful, Counsellor, The mighty God [here is Immanuel], The everlasting Father, The Prince of Peace.''

Much discussion has arisen over the Hebrew noun rendered into English by the word ''virgin.'' It has been pointed out that the word is not the Hebrew for virgin (*bethuleh*), but the Hebrew for young woman (*almah*). An answer to this discussion is found, first, in the usage of this word *almah* throughout the Old Testament. It is used seven times in the Hebrew canon (Genesis 24:43; Song of Solomon 1:3; 6:8; Isaiah 7:14; Exodus 2:8; Proverbs 30:19; Psalm 68:25). It is rendered into English four times as virgin, once as damsel, and twice as maid. In all these references it literally means a marriageable, yet unmarried, young woman. In every instance a virgin is implied. A second answer to this matter is found in the application of Isaiah 7:14, by the Holy Spirit, to

Mary, the mother of Jesus (Matthew 1:22-23).

The New Testament: We have the historical records of the birth of Christ in the Gospels of Matthew and Luke. Both alike insist upon the virginity of Mary.

1. In Matthew (1:1-16) is given the legal genealogy of Christ through His adoptive father, Joseph, going back as far as Abraham. This, of course, proves Him to be the Son of David and heir to the throne of David. It also proves that He is the Hebrew Messiah. Here also is the angelic annunciation of the birth of Jesus to Joseph which places an emphasis upon the humanity of our Lord.

2. In Luke (3:23-38) the genealogy of Christ is traced through His mother, Mary, directly back to Adam. This proves that He is the fulfillment of the prophecy regarding the Seed of the woman (Genesis 3:15). Here the angelic annunciation is to Mary; it places the emphasis upon the deity of the Lord Jesus. He actually is the Son of God. Concerning Him the Father eventually would say, "Thou art My beloved Son; in Thee I am well pleased" (Luke 3:22). Notwithstanding there were many who supposed Him to be only the son of Joseph.

3. For centuries there have been some who believed that the Apostle John makes a strong statement regarding the virgin birth in his Gospel. The King James version reads: "Which were born, not of blood, nor of the will of the flesh, nor of the will of man, but of God" (John 1:13). According to this translation this passage is generally applied to the spiritual birth of those who receive the Lord Jesus as their Saviour. The third chapter of this same Gospel is a complementary part of this portion and concept, "Except a man be born of water and of the Spirit, he cannot enter into the kingdom of God."

According to Tertullian, as early as the second century, there was another reading which he claimed was the original, the correct one. It reads, "Who was born, not of blood, not of the will of the flesh, nor of the will of man, but of God." If this reading is the correct one, then it is a definite reference to the virgin birth of our Lord. It is a concise statement covering His birth as recorded by Matthew and Luke.

There has been much discussion over this passage and different interpretations have been expressed by prominent theologians of both the past and the present. There is one suggestion which seems to harmonize the two readings, the plural and the singular pronouns. It is that the miraculous, physical birth of Christ is an illustration of the spiritual birth of all believers. We have a similar reference in Paul's Epistle to the Ephesians. In the second section of Ephesians 1 the apostle is dealing with the physical resurrection and ascension of the Lord Jesus, and at the beginning of chapter 2 this wonderful demonstration of the power of God demonstrates the power of God in the spiritual resurrection and ascension of the believer.

4. The statement of the Apostle Paul to the Galatians is sometimes quoted as an affirmation of the virgin birth: "God sent forth His Son, made [born, or come] of a woman, made under the law" (Galatians 4:4). Actually this is not a direct reference to the virgin birth of Christ; it merely indicates that the Son of God became human and began life here in the usual way, born of a woman. Notwithstanding, it should be noticed that although the apostle mentions the physical mother of our Lord, he never once mentions a physical father. What eloquent silence!

5. There is one other New Testament passage that ought to be discussed in its relation to the virgin birth of Christ, the application of Psalm 40 to the Lord Jesus in Hebrews 10:5. The Psalm reads, "Sacrifice and offering Thou didst not desire; Mine ears hast Thou opened." (verse 6). The application of this by the Holy Spirit reads, "Sacrifice and offering Thou wouldest not, but a body hast Thou prepared Me."

Before the Lord Jesus could have open ears as a perfect Servant, He had to have a body to which the ears would belong. This passage indicates that the miracle of creation as seen in the case of Adam was repeated in the incarnation of Christ. As God Himself directly formed Adam, so God Himself through the Divine Spirit miraculously formed the body of the Lord Jesus Christ in the womb of the Virgin Mary. ("Hebrews" in the *Greek New Testament* by Kenneth S. Wuest, is a good source of further help.)

These references in the New Testament confirm the faith of the true believer; they demonstrate the vigorous convictions of the apostles in the virgin birth of our Holy Lord.

The Doctrine of the Virgin Birth

After our survey of Scriptures dealing with the virgin birth of Christ, it becomes necessary to formulate a doctrine covering this subject: a systematic outline of teaching relative to the virgin birth and its bearing upon other Biblical themes, many of which are dependent upon it.

The Virgin Birth and Inspiration. Any denial of the virgin birth of Christ is a denial of the veracity, inerrancy, and infallibility of the Bible. The belief that "all Scripture is given by inspiration of God" (2 Timothy 3:16) demands that we give it credence not only in divine revelation but in accurate preservation of all historical records. The Holy Scriptures are God-breathed whether we accept this as in-breathing or out-breathing (inspiration or expiration); the source of the Bible is in God Himself. If one narrative be proved fictitious or even faulty, then the whole may be considered errant and fallible. Faith in the inspiration of the Bible involves the acceptance of it in whole and in parts as having been transmitted by God to man and preserved in its writing by a power beyond that of man.

God is the source, but He has used holy men as His mouthpiece. "Holy men of God spake as they were moved by the Holy Spirit'' (2 Peter 1:21). The Word of God was not given by any personal or particular explanation, nor by the determination of anyone; the holy men who gave us the Book were impelled in their ministry by the Divine Spirit. Through these men God performed the miracle of inspiration; He used holy men, but fallible men, to write an infallible volume, the Holy Scriptures, the Bible.

The Bible is God's witness to us of His presence working throughout human history. The record of the virgin birth given by Matthew and Luke are the revelation of God's great work among men, for men.

Dr. Howard A. Kelly in his book, *A Scientific Man and the Bible,* says concerning the virgin birth and the Scriptures:

> The virgin birth is a fact fully established by competent testimony and abundant collateral evidences, believed by men all through the ages as a necessary factor in their salvation secured by an ever-living, ever-acting Saviour, viewed with wonder by angels in Heaven and acknowledged by the Father. To deny the virgin birth because of its miraculous nature is to deny the validity of all Scripture, which is but a continuous series of revelations of the mind and acts of God, and as such is miraculous throughout.[1]

The Virgin Birth and Christ's Impeccability. There is a statement by the writer of the Epistle to the Hebrews which says of our Lord that He was an High Priest who was ''tempted like as we are, yet without sin.'' This seems to be in conflict with the account of our Lord's temptation by the devil in the wilderness (Matthew 4:1-11; Luke 4:1-13). If sin was not a temptation to Christ was His experience with Satan a real one?

Even a cursory examination of this event in the earthly life of the Lord Jesus requires that we define certain terms, for example, impeccable. Webster's unabridged dictionary gives as the meaning of this word: ''Not liable to sin or wrong doing;

---

[1]Dr. Howard Kelly, *A Scientific Man and the Bible,* page 94.

exempt from the possibility of sinning, as no mere man is impeccable.''

The word ''temptation'' as used in the Bible must be understood. James, the Lord's brother, enlightens us in this connection. Temptation in its Biblical use has a double meaning: first, ''Blessed is the man that endureth temptation'' (James 1:12). In the immediate context this word can only mean ''to be tested.'' The NASV renders this verse, ''Blessed is the man who perseveres under trial.'' The same version translates Genesis 22:1, ''God tested Abraham''; He tried him.

Secondly, James says, ''Every man is tempted when he is drawn away of his own lust, and enticed'' (1:14). Here to tempt is to incite to do evil. This is the usual understanding of the word. The question then arises, and it is only a hypothetical one, if sin was not a temptation to Christ, were the inducements and allurements of the devil a temptation to Him? Could Satan overcome the Last Adam as he had the first (1 Corinthians 15:45)?

That the Lord Jesus was tested by the sinless effects of sin is readily conceded. He knew what it was to be weary, to be thirsty, to be hungry, to be poor, etc. But because of the holy indissoluble union of His two natures, He was impeccable. Since God cannot sin, the Son of God by virtue of His divine essence could not, in spite of the adverse circumstances in which He had to live.

Indubitably Satan attempted to induce the Lord Jesus to sin relative to His Sonship with God: ''If Thou be the Son of God, command that these stones be made bread.'' In the second place he sought to incite the Lord to pride; he tempted Him concerning His Messiahship: ''The devil taketh Him up into the holy city, and setteth Him on a pinnacle of the temple, and said unto Him, If Thou be the Son of God, cast Thyself down: for it is written, He shall give His angels charge over Thee: and in their hands they shall bear Thee up, lest at any time Thou dash Thy foot against a stone.''

Finally, in his wickedness, ''the devil taketh Him up into an exceeding high mountain, and showeth Him all the kingdoms of the world, and the glory of them; and said unto Him, All these will I give Thee, if Thou wilt fall down and worship me.'' This satanic temptation was in regard to world dominion; in regard to His kingship. Thank God, in spite of the malignity and evil, the Lord Jesus Christ is, in the purposes of God, the King of kings and Lord of lords.

The piercing thrusts made by the Word of God were not, as they might first appear, a self-defense by the Lord; they were in very truth rebukes, refutations, rebuttals; self-defense was unnecessary. This is fully demonstrated by the Lord's command, ''Get thee hence, Satan,'' or as it is rendered in the NASV, ''Begone, Satan.'' Even Satan had to bow, obey, and leave the presence of the Lord. Christ was and is absolutely impeccable. To this end was He born the Seed of the woman, the virgin-born Son of Mary who knew no sin and did no sin.

The Virgin Birth and World Dominion. When God created man, He said: ''Be fruitful, and multiply, and replenish the earth, and subdue it: and have dominion over the fish of the sea, and over the fowl of the air, and over every living thing that moveth upon the earth'' (Genesis 1:28). Man was indeed king of the earth. His sovereignty was over the three visible spheres of creation: the sea, the air, and the ground. Adam and Eve in their innocence were co-rulers over all.

Man's origin was divine. Of the vegetable kingdom we read, ''Let the earth bring forth,'' but in contrast, God said, ''Let Us make man in Our image, after Our likeness'' (Genesis 1:26). Man from the very beginning was distinguished from all else in the earthly creation. His divine origin and the sublime dignity of his constitution fitted him for the glory and authority that he was to bear as the head of all. Well might the Psalmist in his creation poem say, "O LORD, how manifold are Thy works! in wisdom hast Thou made them all: the earth is full of Thy riches" (Psalm 104:24).

The Spirit of God through David describes just how God placed man in so exalted a position: "Thou hast made him a little lower than the angels [not a little higher than the beasts], and hast crowned him with glory and honour. Thou madest him to have dominion over the works of Thy hands; Thou hast put all things under his feet. . . . O LORD our Lord, how excellent is Thy name in all the earth!" (Psalm 8:4-9).

Adam was sinless when as a monarch he ruled the world. He was not immune from sin. God had given to him the freedom of choice, the complete control and action of his will. That Adam abused that personal liberty is a historical fact, and thereby he brought sin into the human race (Romans 5:12). Man's honor and power antedated the grievous disaster of the fall.

With the fall, the entrance of sin into the human family, even the earth rebelled against his rule. The guilty pair were no longer co-rulers: "Unto the woman [God] said . . . thy desire shall be to thy husband, and he shall rule over thee" (Genesis 3:16).

The writer of the Epistle to the Hebrews in a very concise and terse statement asserts how the loss of Adam's regal glory resulted in the conditions of the world ever since. "But now we see not yet all things put under him" (Hebrews 2:8). Adam lost his exalted position; he was a complete failure.

Have the purposes of God been nullified? Or will He eventually have a sinless sovereign over all His work? In anticipation of the full accomplishment of His original intention, God has a Last Adam as well as a first. The first Adam was made a living soul. Such was his beginning. Man's origin was divine.

Of the Last Adam it is said, that He was a quickening spirit—a life-giving spirit—(1 Corinthians 15:45). He is the source of life, both spiritual and physical. Of Him it is prophesied, "Behold, one like the Son of man came with the clouds of heaven, and came to the Ancient of days, and they brought Him near before Him. And there was given Him dominion, and glory, and a kingdom, that all people, nations, and languages, should serve Him: His dominion is an everlasting dominion, which shall not . . . be destroyed" (Daniel 7:13-14). "God also hath highly exalted Him, and given Him a name which is above every name: that at the name of Jesus every knee should bow" (Philippians 2:9-10). The debacle of sin in Eden, that sad event in man's early history, will never be repeated for the Eternal Universal Sovereign is impeccable, "In Him is no sin" (1 John 3:5).

"For unto us a child is born [of the Virgin Mary], unto us a son is given [from the Eternal Father]: and the government shall be upon His shoulder: and His name shall be called Wonderful, Counsellor, The mighty God, The everlasting Father, The Prince of Peace. Of the increase of His government and peace there shall be no end, upon the throne of David, and upon His kingdom to order it, and to establish it with judgment and with justice from henceforth even forever. The zeal of the LORD of hosts will perform this" (Isaiah 9:6-7).

Great God of wonders! all Thy ways
  Display Thine attributes divine;
But the bright glories of Thy grace
  Above Thine other wonders shine:
Who is a pardoning God like Thee?
  Or who has grace so rich and free?

SAMUEL DAVIES

3

THE GOD-MAN

To speak of Jesus as a sinless man or even as a perfect man is to describe inadequately the personality of the Lord Jesus Christ. We must remember that Adam was a sinless man for the early part of his life; for just how long we are not informed. Adam was a perfect man until seduced by Satan through Eve.

Sound Biblical doctrine asserts that in one person, the Lord Jesus, there are two natures which are complete in themselves, and these are organically and indissolubly united. Dr. Strong in his *Systematic Theology* states:

> Orthodox doctrine forbids us to either divide the person or confound the natures. . . . The two natures are bound together . . . by a bond unique and inscrutable, which constitutes them one person with a single consciousness and will, this consciousness and will including within their possible range both the human and the divine.[1]

This exceptional personality is spoken of as the mystery of God, even Christ (Colossians 2:2 RV).

The word mystery occurs some twenty times in the writings of the apostle to the Gentiles. They make reference to numerous details in the eternal purposes of God. Mysteries actually were hidden secrets. To Daniel the secret of Nebuchadnezzar's dream was revealed. This was a description of God's counsel concerning the nations. In the earlier ages of human history, many of His secrets God did not make

---

[1]Strong, *Systematic Theology*, page 673.

known unto the sons of men (Ephesians 3:5). Prophets of Old Testament times inquired and searched diligently to discover what the Spirit of God testified of the sufferings of Christ and the glory that was to follow. This ministry of the Holy Spirit was related to God's plans of complete redemption (1 Peter 1:10-11).

In God's own time He revealed mysteries to His holy apostles and prophets, New Testament prophets (Ephesians 3:3-5). These His servants then communicated the mysteries to the Church. The fervent wish of the Apostle Paul was that all the Colossians, and of course all other Christians, might attain to the full knowledge of the mystery which is Christ. He, our blessed Lord, is the revelation of all God's secrets, yet He Himself in many respects is incomprehensible to our puny minds. Who can understand the mysteries of the incarnation? Who can know the hidden facts of His personality? Who can possibly fathom the depths of the Lord's accomplishment on the cross at Calvary?

It is necessary that all recognize that the personality of the Lord Jesus is incomprehensible. "Great is the mystery of godliness: God was manifest in the flesh" (1 Timothy 3:16). Kent, in his exposition *The Pastoral Epistles,* affirms:

> Although His [Christ's] Deity was often veiled during His ministry, at times the veil was lifted and pronouncement was made that the incarnate Jesus was the divine Son of God, and was absolutely righteous. Such occurred at the baptism (Matthew 3:15-17); transfiguration (Matthew 17:5, cf., 2 Peter 1:16-18); resurrection (Romans 1:4); ascension (John 16:10), and other less prominent occasions.[1]

Consequently there are Bible students who speak and write of Him as the God-Man. He is the perfect Man, the true God, the one Christ.

---

[1]Homer A. Kent, *The Pastoral Epistles,* page 146.

While sinlessness indicates the absence of sin, impeccability indicates incapability to sin. Christ was not subject to sin in any form, for by His holy nature He was immune to sin. The truth of the impeccability of Christ rests upon the fact that Christ was not able to sin, not upon the idea that Christ was able not to sin.

His Incarnation

The study of the incarnation of the Lord involves many pertinent details. In examining them we must be cautious in our endeavors to explain the mystery of the One who possessed both Godhood and Manhood. The Bible presents these truths in type, prophecy, history, and doctrine.

Inasmuch as most are thoroughly acquainted with the historical records of the birth of our Lord, we shall consider other minute details found in the well-chosen language of the New Testament. These details are revealed in the verbs and proper nouns used in direct connection with the incarnation of God in Christ.

The verbs. It is difficult to consider these in proper sequence; this we do not know. Consequently the order in which they are mentioned is merely suggestive.

First, the passive verbs. These are verbs which indicate that in certain details of the incarnation Christ was passive.

(a) He was sent by the authority of the Father (John 17:21; Galatians 4:4; Romans 8:3). The concept of the Father sending His Son is of great importance to the Apostle John. He makes reference to this both in his Gospel and in his first Epistle. Through the testimony of the Church, the world is to believe that God sent Him (John 17:21,23). John further states that God sent His Son to be the Saviour of the world, the propitiation for our sins, and that we might have life through Him (1 John 4:9-14).

(b) Christ was made flesh by the power and influence of the Holy Spirit (John 1:14; Luke 1:35).

(c) He was born of the blessed Virgin Mary (Matthew 2:1-10; Luke 2:1-7).

(d) He was given by the Father (John 3:16). Furthermore He gave Himself. Each believer may say, "The Son of God . . . loved me, and gave Himself for me" (Galatians 2:20).

(e) He was manifested for us men (1 Peter 1:18-21; 1 John 3:5,8).

Secondly, the active verbs. These verbs suggest the personal actions of the Lord Jesus relative to His incarnation.

(a) He emptied Himself of the positional glories and the outward insignia of deity (Philippians 2:7-8). He did not empty Himself of deity. "For in Him dwelleth all the fullness of the Godhead bodily" (Colossians 2:9).

(b) He humbled Himself (Philippians 2:8).

(c) He came into the world to save sinners (1 Timothy 1:15). In so doing He could say, "Lo, I come (in the volume of the book it is written of Me,) to do Thy will, O God" (Hebrews 10:7).

(d) He was obedient unto death (Philippians 2:8; Hebrews 5:8). He was not obedient to the summons of death, but obedient to the will of His Father to the extent of dying in ignominy and shame, for the ungodly.

The proper nouns. There are several appellations and names given our Lord which are directly connected with His incarnation. These reveal different facets of His personal glories.

(a) He is called "that holy thing" in relation to the fact that He was born immaculately (Luke 1:35).

(b) He is designated "the Son of God" and "the Son of the Highest" in connection with His trinitarian relationship (Luke 1:32).

(c) He is called "Emmanuel" as to His deity (Matthew 1:23).

(d) The name "Jesus" was given directly in connection with His humanity (Luke 1:31).

(e) He is spoken of as "the Word" for He is not only the expression of a specific revelation, He is that revelation (John 1:1,14).

(f) In like manner Christ is called "the image of the invisible God" for He was and ever will be the visible representative of the invisible God (Colossians 1:15; Hebrews 1:3). He very definitely was the Son of God (John 1:18, 34). It was for this claim, which the Jews said was blasphemy, that Christ was executed (John 19:7).

Some eighty times the Lord Jesus called Himself "the Son of Man." In this He has given us a commentary on Daniel 7:13-14. It may be said that many excellent expositors of the Holy Scriptures consider the title Son of Man as Messianic, teaching that it refers to our Lord Jesus as the Anointed One, who as the Last Adam shall rule the world.

This word study of verbs and nouns presents a rather detailed doctrine of the incarnation of the Lord. It not only describes who became incarnate but how and why. This same word study if pursued farther will reveal what Christ was, what He became, what He did, what He is doing now, and what He eventually will do.

Christ's True Humanity

It is well known that the four Gospels—Matthew, Mark, Luke, and John—give a fourfold portrait of the Lord Jesus in His perfect manhood. While the blessed subject is the same in all four, each Gospel pictures Him in a slightly different aspect, an aspect that must be viewed through His humanity. In Matthew, Christ is seen in His perfect humanity as King; in Mark, as a slave; in Luke, as a cultured gentleman, probably a physician; in John He is viewed as God manifest in the flesh.

Inasmuch as Luke's point of emphasis is the perfect sinless man, Christ Jesus, we might expect certain descriptive details which are not found elsewhere, and in this we are not disappointed.

He is seen as a babe. The announcement of the angels to the shepherds was, "Ye shall find the babe wrapped in swaddling clothes, lying in a manger" (Luke 2:12). The angels did not command the shepherds that they go and seek this remarkable babe, they assumed that they would do so; consequently they gave these humble men a sign by which the Lord would be revealed to them. The first time that the eyes of strangers saw God incarnate, they saw Him as a babe in a cave stable at Bethlehem. What wonderful condescension on the part of God Almighty! "Thus saith the high and lofty One that inhabiteth eternity, whose name is Holy; I dwell in the high and holy place, with him also that is of a contrite and humble spirit, to revive the spirit of the humble, and to revive the heart of the contrite ones" (Isaiah 57:15).

Simeon was one of the few who saw the Lord in His infancy. He with a few others expected that in his day the Lord Christ would appear. The fulfillment of this divine promise is here recorded. Simeon therefore provides us with an example of the many who today expect the imminent return in power and great glory of that blessed One, the King of kings and Lord of lords (Luke 2:25-34; Revelation 19:11-16).

The attitude of Herod was a paradigm of the state of the Jews at the birth of Christ and, of course, their attitude all during His public life and ministry. What he attempted to do, to destroy our Saviour in His infancy, the Jews ultimately did; they crucified Him.

How different was the attitude of the princes from the Orient. Did they gather their hope and knowledge from the signs of the zodiac? Reference has already been made to these signs. Did God Himself guide these men by means of what has been called the miracle star? Perhaps!

The One discovered by these wise men is called "the young child." He no longer is a babe as he was when found by the shepherds. Furthermore, they did not find Him in a stable but in a house. The stable was a temporary measure in the hour of emergency. From the stable they must have moved into the house.

Inasmuch as wicked Herod in his fury ordered the destruction of all children in Bethlehem from two years old and under it is assumed that the young child worshiped by the wise men was probably nearly two years of age (Matthew 2:1-18).

We must bear in mind that the early Church knew why Christ had been born and had died before it knew the manner of His immaculate birth. The Church had Paul's Epistles before it had any of the four Gospels. It would seem that the Holy Spirit indited the four Gospels in order to produce the earthly history of the Lord Jesus, whom the Church only knew in doctrine. The accomplishments in redemption of the life, death, and resurrection of Christ were well known throughout the world before His biography was written.

In the Epistles the apostles deal chiefly with the life of Christ after His baptism. They knew very little of His former experiences, but they had been witnesses of much that transpired during the years of His public life and ministry.

There is only one event in the boyhood of Christ that is recorded; that is when, as a boy of twelve years, He appeared among the doctors in the Temple. As a child the Lord may have gone to Jerusalem each year with Joseph and Mary. Of course, this occasion may have been considered very important and in preparation for His thirteenth year, the year when a Jewish boy reaches his Bar Mitzvah, the year when he becomes a responsible member of the Jewish community. Following this interesting event, there is no further record of a public appearance of the Lord Jesus for eighteen years. During these years He lived in total obscurity.

Dean Farrar says in regard to the early life of Christ:

> There is, then, for the most part a deep silence in the Evangelists respecting this period; but what eloquence in their silence! May we find in their very reticence a wisdom and an instruction more profound than if they had filled many volumes with minor details.[1]

Furthermore, Farrar despises the Apocryphal Gospels, as they are called:

> We have only to turn to the Apocryphal Gospels to find how different is the false human ideal from the divine fact.

One of these apocryphal gospels is called the Gospel of St. Thomas and was written sometime during the second century. It deals with the infancy of Christ and gives accounts of the miracles of His boyhood. These are all fraudulent, heretical, and repulsive.

The final stage of natural development is seen throughout much of Luke's Gospel. Christ is seen as a mature person in His manhood, a vigorous and dynamic personality in His early thirties.

The true humanity of Christ was predetermined. In the counsels of the Godhead, "Christ [was] as a lamb without blemish and without spot: who verily was foreordained before the foundation of the world" (1 Peter 1:19-20; Acts 4:28).

Satan in the Holy Scriptures is pictured as a roaring lion walking about seeking whom He may devour (1 Peter 5:8). On the cross the Lord Jesus was the patient, defenseless Lamb in the wicked and cruel jaws of the devil, a rapacious monster.

---

[1]F. W. Farrar, *The Life of Christ,* pages 25-26.

The old serpent, Satan, for a moment appeared to be victorious, but Calvary was his final hour, there his power was broken. By the weakness and the meekness, yet by the mighty, eternal power of the Lamb of God, Satan was overcome.

The Lord Jesus was the Lamb of God in that God provided Him. In infinite love and grace God provided Him as the sacrifice for human guilt, the one sacrifice for man's acceptance with God. Those who know its values and perpetual efficacy will join in loud acclaim: "Thou art Worthy . . . for Thou wast slain, and hast redeemed us to God by Thy blood out of every kindred, and tongue, and people, and nation" (Revelation 5:9).

The true humanity of Christ was prophesied. Isaiah here sings a song for Israel (Isaiah 9:6-7). Her glorious future is described earlier in this same chapter where he speaks of joy after harvest, freedom after bondage, and peace after war. Such liberty, such tranquility for poor Israel! All because a real nobleman has been born, an eternal Son has been given. In regal power and honor He is seen seated on the throne of His father David, judging the twelve tribes of Israel. The kingdom has been restored to Israel under the supremacy of the Man Christ Jesus.

Isaiah gives further information regarding this great Sovereign. He speaks of Him as a Branch out of the roots of Jesse (Isaiah 11:1-6). Jeremiah in his sadness anticipated not only the restoration of the captive nation, Israel, but also that through her and her King there would be world-wide integrity, prosperity, and dominion: "Behold, the days come, saith the LORD, that I will raise unto David a righteous Branch, and a King shall reign and prosper, and shall execute judgment and justice in the earth. In His day Judah shall be saved, and Israel shall dwell safely: and this is His name whereby He shall be called, THE LORD OUR RIGHTEOUSNESS" (Jeremiah 23:5-6).

The Spirit of God leaves no doubt in our minds about the interpretation of Isaiah 53. The Ethiopian diplomat, as he read this unique passage from the Old Testament, inquired of Philip, "Of whom speaketh the prophet this? of himself, or of some other man? Then Philip opened his mouth, and began at the same scripture, and preached unto him Jesus" (Acts 8:34-35).

In spite of the modern Jewish interpretation which applies these words (Isaiah 53) of the prophet to their nation in its grief, rejection, and suffering, the clear understanding of the portion is its application to an individual: scorned, unjustly condemned, crucified as a criminal, and threatened with an ignoble burial; yet buried as a nobleman by noblemen. Here, to use the concept implied by Philip, the crucifixion of Jesus is carefully delineated.

The Old Testament prophets spoke of the coming of a personal, human Messiah King.

During the eighteen silent years, as we speak of them, "Jesus increased in wisdom and stature, and in favour with God and man" (Luke 2:52). We assume that Jesus became a carpenter and in the shop helped to provide for his brothers and sisters (Matthew 13:55-56). In all probability we are correct in supposing that Joseph died and left Mary a widow with a family of boys and girls. Perhaps Jesus, being the eldest, sought to provide the help and leadership of which the fatherless family had been deprived by the death of Joseph.

In the personality of our Lord, as viewed from the human perspective, there was a mental development as well as a physical development. Let it be affirmed that in each stage of growth there was perfection, a perfection in boyhood as well as in manhood. "In [Him] are hid all the treasures of wisdom and knowledge" (Colossians 2:3).

Not only did our Lord develop physically, but in that state He frequently suffered. He hungered (Matthew 4:1-11). He grew weary and sat upon the curbing of Jacob's well. He became thirsty and asked for a drink of water (John 4:6-7). He wept (John 11:35). He sweat (Luke 22:44).

That His emotions were frequently aroused is well evidenced by the divinely appointed authors of the four Gospels. On one sabbath day, when about to heal a man with a withered hand, because His enemies criticized Him for doing good "He looked about on them with anger being grieved for the hardness of their hearts" (Mark 3:5). Through His omniscience He knew their thoughts. Notwithstanding, His omnipotence was present to heal. They would hinder if possible, but they could not staunch the blessing.

On another occasion the Lord was moved with compassion for two blind men so that He touched their eyes; and immediately they received sight (Matthew 20:34).

Deity clothed in humanity was with the people, but only faith could say, "We beheld His glory," the mystery of His Majesty.

Dr. B. B. Warfield gives a word of caution:

> We can never hope to comprehend how the infinite God and finite humanity can be united in one single person; and it is very easy to go fatally astray in attempting to explain the interactions in the unitary person of natures so diverse from one another.[1]

Like the Psalmist we might challenge our souls, saying "He is thy Lord; worship thou Him" (Psalm 45:11).

An explanatory paragraph from Dr. Walvoord's volume, *Jesus Christ our Lord,* should be inserted here:

> The union of the two natures in Christ is related vitally to His acts as an incarnate person. Though the divine nature was immutable, the human nature could suffer and learn through experience with the result that the corporate person could be said to come into new experiences. Thus Christ learned by suffering (Hebrews 5:8). In a similar way, the act of redemption in which

---

[1]B. B. Warfield, *The Person and Work of Christ,* page 69.

Christ offered Himself a sacrifice for sin was an act of His whole person. It was traceable to both natures, not to the human nature alone nor to the divine. As man Christ could die, but only as God could His death have infinite value sufficient to provide redemption for the sins of the whole world. Thus the human blood of Christ has eternal and infinite value because it was shed as part of the divine-human person.[1]

Heresies About the Personality of Christ

This seems the appropriate time to call attention to some of the heresies regarding the personality of the God-Man, the Lord Jesus Christ.

Speculative theology accepts what is known as the Kenosis theory. This theory attempts to elucidate the silence of Scripture. The Word of God does not state of what Christ emptied Himself; the important fact lies in what he became by so doing.

Dr. Tatford clearly states the Kenosis theory and just as clearly states the objections of orthodox Christianity to its contentions.

> The kenotic theory is that Christ "emptied" Himself of His Godhead and consequently His divine attributes (and not merely of the use of them) when He became incarnate. The Philippian passage, as James Orr says, is "taken to mean that, during His earthly life, the Son ceased to exist in the form of God even as respects His heavenly existence. The place of the Son in the life of the Godhead was for the time suspended." As Orr pertinently remarks, "The difficulties in the way of this conception of the temporary obliteration of consciousness and activity on the part of one of the members of the Holy Trinity appear insuperable." He could not have divested Himself of the inner reality of Deity, even if He surrendered its outward manifestation. Moreover, Vincent maintains that the word "emptied" in Philippians 2:7 cannot possibly

---

[1]John F. Walvoord, *Jesus Christ Our Lord,* page 120.

indicate "surrender of Deity or paralysis of Deity, nor a change of personality, nor a break in continuity of self-consciousness."

Of what then did the Son empty Himself, since renunciation of His deity would have been a denial of His own nature? He laid aside the glory He shared with the Father in a past eternity (John 17:5). He divested Himself of the external insignia of His dignity and majesty. While never ceasing to be what He ever was, He veiled the blazing light of eternity to reveal Himself in flesh.[1]

The Lord Jesus while on earth was fully aware of His relationship to God. This was clearly revealed at His baptism (Matthew 3:15-17). He was thus conscious of His deity and He likewise was fully cognizant that He was man, perfect man.

Furthermore, He had a complete insight into His mission and work. In the upper room it is recorded by John, "Jesus knew that His hour was come that He should depart out of this world unto the Father, having loved His own which were in the world, He loved them unto the end. . . . Jesus knowing that the Father had given all things into His hands, and that He was come from God, and went to God; He riseth from supper" (John 13:1-4).

The only honest deduction in regard to the apparent limitations in the life and ministry of the God-Man is that these were self-imposed and temporary.

Heresies revived from ancient times. Arianism (Arius, A.D. 256?-336) denies the eternal deity of Christ; it teaches that He preexisted before His birth at Bethlehem, but that He was only God's first and highest creature. It teaches that in the incarnation this highest of all God's creatures was made visible to mankind, but that He never claimed to be God. Arianism is the basic heresy of the Jehovah Witnesses.

Apollinarianism (Apollinarius, A.D. 390) teaches that Christ became the Son of God at His birth by Mary, and that

---

[1]Fredk. A. Tatford, *Prophet of Messiah's Advent,* page 105.

His humanity was the same as that of an ordinary man, only His soul was divine.

Nestorianism (Nestorius, A.D. 450). This deceptive heresy teaches that Christ was two persons rather than only one possessing two natures. It asserts that there were times when the man in Christ acted and other times when the God in Christ acted. In other words, Nestorianism believes that our Lord Jesus was a dual personality.

Gnosticism. This heresy appeared toward the close of the apostolic era. It came into the Church with a regrettable force and influence, quickly developing into a dangerous heresy. John apparently, by the divine Spirit, anticipated its sway and made reference to those who denied that the Lord Jesus had come in actual flesh (1 John 2:22; 4:2-3).

The name Gnostic implies that these heretics professed to possess a superior secret knowledge. Peter and John probably had their boast in mind when they repeatedly made mention of the Christian's full knowledge. Each believer is to grow in grace and in the full knowledge of our Lord and Saviour Jesus Christ (2 Peter 3:18).

These then are some of the ancient heresies which attempted to divert attention away from the God-Man.

4

THE FULLNESS OF THE GODHEAD

The logic of the postapostolic Ebionites (Gnostics) was humanly clear but humanly very deceptive. They argued that since God was so mighty, transcendent, and immense, He could not be contained nor confined within the limits of a small fragile and impotent body. They therefore denied the true full humanity of the Lord Jesus Christ. They intimated that the human body of our Lord was a fantasy, a mystical wonder. Their heresy was condemned by early Church counsels.

To deny the deity of our Lord they inverted their reasoning. They said, Inasmuch as humanity is so frail and impoverished, Deity with all its activities of the personal and moral attributes could never enter and remain in such a weak, deficient vehicle. Consequently they rejected the absolute Godhead of the Lord Jesus.

Human investigations and conclusions which ignore "the mystery of God, and of the Father, and of Christ" (Colossians 2:2), can be wholly erroneous. Paul's statement to the Colossians has been rendered by some translators somewhat differently: "The mystery of God, even Christ." A pregnant comment has been made upon this statement: the full exercise of the believer's intelligence should result in the true knowledge of the mystery of God. This is the secret that God is willing to disclose for the full enjoyment of His own.

While the Gnostics were not recognized as a cult until some time after the death of the Apostle John, the seeds of their heresy were planted in the hearts of some. By thus imbibing this heterodoxy many became apostates. It was of these that John wrote, "They [the many antichrists of verse 18] went out from us, but they were not of us; for had they been of us, they would no doubt have continued with us: but they went out, that they might be made manifest that they were not all of us" (1 John 2:19).

"I am extremely sad," said an elder of a large assembly to another Christian. "It was my duty this morning, according to 1 Timothy 1:18-19, to expel a young man from our church fellowship. I have known him from his birth. While still quite young he professed to receive the Lord Jesus as his Saviour. I fear that recently he has absorbed vain philosophies of science falsely so-called. I hope and pray that he is not actually an apostate, and that he will soon discover his mistake and return again to the Lord."

"May it be so," responded the sympathetic and understanding friend.

How many useful lives have been marred! How many Christian relatives and friends have been hurt! And how much grief has been brought upon the Church by Gnosticism in one form or another!

It is because of this hazard that the Apostle John calls attention to certain tests regarding the personality of the Lord Jesus. The first in regard to His real, physical humanity. He gives this test in both a positive and a negative form: "Every spirit that confesseth that Jesus Christ is come in the flesh is of God: and every spirit that confesseth not that Jesus Christ is come in the flesh is not of God: and this is that spirit of antichrist" (1 John 4:2-3). Hereby we know the Spirit of God. The heretical Gnostic professed a superior intellect, a more accurate knowledge. John apparently is insisting that, in contrast, the Christian has the superior knowledge because he knows the Spirit of God: "Now we have received, not the spirit of the world, but the Spirit which is of God; that we might know the things that are freely given to us of God'' (1 Corinthians 2:12). The more excellent knowledge subscribes to the perfect, sinless humanity of the Lord Jesus Christ.

The second test is concerning Christ's essential nature: ''Whosoever shall confess that Jesus is the Son of God, God dwelleth in him, and he in God'' (1 John 4:15).

We know that the Lord Jesus was fully conscious of His divine origin, His divine destiny, and His divine power: ''Jesus knowing that the Father had given all things into His hands, and that He was come from God, and went to God'' (John 13:3). But there were other facts of which He was likewise constantly aware. He was absolutely cognizant of His real humanity.

The Lord intimated this repeatedly in the language that He used. For example, to critical Jews, who afterwards took up stones to stone Him, He affirmed ''Now ye seek to kill Me, a man that hath told you the truth, which I have heard of God'' (John 8:40).

At Caesarea Philippi Peter boldly declared, ''Thou art the Christ, the Son of the living God.'' And the Lord replied, ''Blessed art thou, Simon Barjona: for flesh and blood [My bodily appearance] hath not revealed it unto thee, but My Father which is in heaven'' (Matthew 16:16-17). These words bear a very probable relevance to His physical image.

Later as He instituted the Lord's Supper, He made a further important reference to His humanity: ''He took bread, and gave thanks, and brake it, and gave unto them, saying, This is My body which is given for you: this do in remembrance of Me. Likewise also the cup after supper, saying, This cup is the new testament in My blood, which is shed for you'' (Luke 22:19-20). These precious elements were symbols of blessed physical realities.

As the Lord anticipated His going to die at Calvary, He

disclosed His feelings: "My soul is exceeding sorrowful, even unto death" (Matthew 26:38).

After His resurrection, He showed His hands and His side to the disciples (John 20:20). He then said, "Handle Me, and see; for a spirit hath not flesh and bones, as ye see Me have. . . . He showed them His hands and His feet" (Luke 24:39-40). With such extensive evidence, it would be blatant incredulity to cast any uncertainty upon the full knowledge of the Lord Jesus concerning His perfect, immaculate humanity.

Two of the men who had been called to be disciples, men who knew Him as no other humans ever did, believed fully that He was in flesh the manifestation of God. Peter in his pentecostal address spoke of the Lord as "Jesus of Nazareth, a man approved of God" (Acts 2:22). John the disciple who lay closer to Jesus than any of his fellow-disciples at the last supper, many years later recorded: "The Word [The Eternal Word—John 1:1-2] was made flesh, and dwelt among us" (John 1:14). He knew that it was real and pure humanity that reclined beside him in the upper room. It was such experiences that enabled him to write with conviction, "Every spirit that confesseth that Jesus Christ is come in the flesh is of God" (1 John 4:2).

Irenaeus (A.D. 120-202), who was a disciple of the Apostle John and an ardent opponent of the Gnostics, wrote concerning our Lord Jesus Christ:

> For man He wrought His redemptive work, displaying God to man, and man to God. He safeguarded the invisibility of the Father, lest man should become contemptuous of God. . . . At the same time He displayed God in visible form to men through His many acts of mediation, lest man should be utterly remote from God and so cease to be. . . . If the manifestation of God in creation gives life to all who live on earth, much more does the revelation of the Father through the Word bestow life on those who see God.[1]

---

[1]Henry Bettenson, *The Early Christian Fathers*, page 103.

The Lord was certainly conscious of His humanity, and so were many who observed Him as He moved among them for He conducted Himself as a normal man. He hungered (Matthew 4:2), He was thirsty (John 19:28; 4:6), He slept (Matthew 8:24), He was wearied (John 4:6), He wept (John 11:35), He prayed (Matthew 14:23), He had compassion (Matthew 9:36), He loved (Mark 10:21), He became angry (Mark 3:5). These are all the actions and attitudes of an ordinary human being.

Traditional Christianity claims that in the one glorious personality, Jesus Christ the Lord, two natures, the human and the divine, are indivisibly united. He who was actually human was also totally divine. If ever a doctrinal summary was felt necessary there was no need to formulate one, for an authoritative statement is given in the Holy Scriptures: "For in Him dwelleth all the fullness of the Godhead bodily" (Colossians 2:9).

Bishop J. B. Lightfoot makes this poignant comment:

> Paul tells us in Romans (1:20) how God's eternal power and divinity revealed themselves by the light of nature to the heathen mind, but of Immanuel, that in Him dwelleth all the fullness of the Godhead embodied. The hand of omnipotence may be traced in the countless orbs that bespangle the heavens, and in the marvelous coadjustments of our comparatively tiny globe; but in the Son we behold the face of God unveiled, the express image and transcript of His very being.

While our Lord was on earth, on three different occasions from the heavens God the Father acknowledged Him as His Son, and He thus attested to His deity.

The first occasion was at His baptism, near the beginning of His public service. After His baptism Jesus saw Heaven opened, and the Spirit of God descending like a dove, and lighting upon Him. "And there came a voice from heaven saying, Thou art My beloved Son, in whom I am well pleased" (Matthew 3:16-17; Mark 1:10; Luke 3:22; John 1:32-34). Here there is perfect accord between Heaven and earth.

On the mount of transfiguration the same voice was again heard, this time by Peter, James, and John, three disciples filled with awe. This voice expressed full recognition to the Eternal Son. To this more private revelation, the Father added, "Hear ye Him." This would be a call for them not only to listen to Christ, but to acknowledge His superiority by dutiful submission.

At the end of Christ's earthly life and gracious ministry, as the fanatical opposition was reaching its climax, knowing that crucifixion lay just before Him, the Lord Jesus prayed, "Father, save Me from this hour; but for this cause came I unto this hour. . . . Then came there a voice from heaven, saying, I have both glorified it, and will glorify it again. The people therefore that stood by, and heard it, said that it thundered: others said, An angel spake to Him" (John 12:27-29).

The designation "son," used in these heavenly endorsements, among the Hebrews did not necessarily refer to origin or subordination. For example, Barnabas was called "a son of consolation," the two brothers James and John were called "sons of thunder." The Lord Jesus many, many times called Himself, "The Son of man," not only because of His humanity, but because of His future glory (Daniel 7:13). He will eventually do what the first man failed to do. He will rule the whole earth as Son of man, King of kings, and Lord of lords.

It would seem as if, when Jesus of Nazareth was rejected as the Son of God, the Eternal Father both publicly and privately declared this relationship. He attested to the fact by emphasizing, "This is My beloved Son, in whom I am well pleased."

If Heaven was thus ever ready to reveal the deity of Christ to man, the majority of earth was not ready to receive that repeated revelation. Men rejected the claims of Christ and refused to accept the evidences of His supernatural power, the signs, the wonders, and the divers miracles.

One Sabbath day the Lord healed an invalid man, and brought down upon Himself the anger of the Jews: "The Jews sought the more to kill Him, because He had not only broken the sabbath, but said also that God was His Father, making Himself equal with God" (John 5:17-18). Supernatural proofs and divine claims obviously were understood, but they were spurned.

The family in which our Saviour was raised apparently divided over this same personal claim of Christ. We read, "Neither did His brothers believe on Him" (John 7:5). Although He had brothers: James, Joses, Simon, and Judas, and at least two sisters (Matthew 13:55-56) none of them appeared at His crucifixion. They left their mother destitute to face that dreadful ordeal. They manifested that they did not believe that He was the Son of God, the Messiah of Israel. The family was not converted until after the Lord appeared unto James, consequent to His resurrection (1 Corinthians 15:7). A precious picture of that converted and united family is seen in the upper room on the eve of Pentecost: "These [the disciples] all continued with one accord in prayer and supplication, with the women, and Mary the mother of Jesus, and with His brethren" (Acts 1:13-14).

When relating to the people the parable of the Good Shepherd and the sheep, to impress upon His listeners the security of His own, the Lord Jesus said, "My Father, which gave them Me, is greater than all; and no man is able to pluck them out of My Father's hand. I and My Father are one" (John 10:29-30).

Never was Jewish hatred more fierce. "The Jews took up

stones again to stone Him." Well might the Lord demand of these: "Many good works have I showed you from My Father; for which of those works do you stone Me?" In their reply one can almost sense venom in their words: "For a good work we stone Thee not; but for blasphemy; and because that Thou, being a man, makest Thyself God" (John 10:31-33).

There can be no question that the Lord Jesus claimed to have a personal and permanent relationship with God the Father. This is the charge that was laid against Him at His trial before Pilate. His enemies argued before the governor: "We have a law, and by our law He ought to die, because He made Himself the Son of God" (John 19:7). The Jews were determined to ignore all the physical and convincing proofs (many of them performed in their presence) of His deity. This certainly was not true of the men who knew Him best.

The Apostle John, while recording explanations, narratives, dialogues, and quotations, inserted among all this variety of materials his own understanding of the personality of the Lord: "No man hath seen God at any time; the only begotten Son, which is in the bosom of the Father, He hath declared Him" (John 1:18). According to some erudite Greek scholars, for example Westcott and Hort, this verse should read, "God only begotten, who is in the bosom of the Father, He hath declared Him." John the apostle of love sincerely believed in the deity of His Master, the Lord Jesus Christ. Vincent comments on this rendering: " 'God only begotten' indicates the One who was both God and the Only Begotten." In His divine essence Christ was God, in His eternal relationship with the Father He was Son.

There were times when the Lord rebuked His disciple Peter, times when He warned him, times when He instructed him, but there was one occasion when He definitely blessed him. Peter had made the bold assertion concerning the Lord, "Thou art the Christ, the Son of the living God" (Matthew

16:16). The evidence had been seen, the fact had penetrated Peter's Jewish mind. In a contemplative mood, he now freely expressed himself, his Master was indeed, "the Son of the living God." Then what a disclosure on the part of the Lord Jesus: "Blessed art thou, Simon Barjona, for flesh and blood hath not revealed it unto thee, but My Father which is in heaven" (Matthew 16:17).

Whatever the doubts were that deprived Thomas of the blessed experience of the Lord's first appearance among His own after the resurrection, we do not know. Had he come to doubt the Messiahship of Jesus? Or was it even more serious, had he come to doubt the deity of the Master? Whatever was the condition of his mind is open to conjecture. When invited by the Lord to apply the tests that he himself had intimated: "Except I shall see in His hand the print of the nails, and put my finger into the print of the nail, and thrust my hand into His side, I will not believe," all doubts immediately vanished before the incontrovertible proofs, and the incredulous disciple exclaimed, "My Lord and My God" (John 20:24-28). Here we have an involuntary articulation, an ardent ascription to the Lord Jesus of absolute Deity. All skepticism had disappeared and Thomas became a converted and convinced worshiper.

It would seem very improper not to include a statement from that great apostle extraordinary, Paul. There is little doubt that his name will appear on one of the twelve foundations of the New Jerusalem (Revelation 21:14). While he may not have known Christ in the flesh, he saw Him in His glory on the road to Damascus (Acts 9). Because of his profound concern for his fellow-Israelites, and because of the many exceptional privileges which they had received, he avers, "Of [from] whom as concerning the flesh Christ came, who is over all, God blessed for ever. Amen" (Romans 9:5).

The writer of the Epistle to the Hebrews in emphasizing

the deity of Christ directly applies the words of Psalm 45 to the Son, who is superior to angels: "Thy throne, O God, is for ever and ever: the sceptre of Thy kingdom is a right sceptre. Thou lovest righteousness, and hatest wickedness; therefore God, Thy God, hath anointed Thee with the oil of gladness above Thy fellows" (Psalm 45:6-7; Hebrews 1:8-9).

Dr. Griffith Thomas in his excellent little volume, *Christianity is Christ,* argues correctly that the miracles of the Lord were not performed primarily as evidences of His divine power. They were rather just what might be expected from divinity. Since Christ is God, none need be surprised that He did the works of God. Christ Himself was the greatest of all miracles. Every aspect of His life was miraculous.

Moreover, there is a difference between reading the account of a miracle and actually seeing one. Any real proof of the supernatural in the life of the Lord Jesus would impress primarily the observers. What then was the reaction upon the minds of those who saw the actual miracles performed by the Lord?

On one occasion a great multitude came to Jesus bringing with them "those that were lame, blind, dumb, maimed, and many others, and cast them down at Jesus' feet; and He healed them: Insomuch that the multitude wondered, when they saw the dumb to speak, the maimed to be whole, the lame to walk, and the blind to see: and they glorified the God of Israel" (Matthew 15:30-31). Surely the common people rejoiced in His power.

When the Lord came down from the mount of transfiguration, a distraught father brought his lunatic boy to the Lord, saying, "Master, I beseech Thee, look upon my son: for he is mine only child. . . . Jesus answering said, O faithless and perverse generation, how long shall I be with you, and suffer you? Bring thy son hither. . . . And Jesus rebuked the unclean spirit, and healed the child, and delivered him again to his father. And they were all amazed at the mighty power of God'' (Luke 9:37-43).

If the devil on this occasion sought to demonstrate his great power over the human mind and body, and if he attempted to destroy the sublimity and fame of the Lord Jesus, he completely failed. Nevertheless, the Lord knew how fickle humanity is and that eventually the general attitude of approval would be altered.

It is not surprising that it is in this context that the Lord Jesus said to His disciples, ''Let these sayings sink down into your ears: for the Son of Man shall be delivered into the hands of men.''

The stupidity and the incredulity of man are inconceivable. The reaction to the resurrection of Lazarus bewilders one. ''The chief priests consulted that they might put Lazarus also to death; because by reason of him many of the Jews went away, and believed on Jesus'' (John 12:10-11).

Many were attracted to Christ through the resurrection of Mary's brother, but the hatred and the anger of the chief priests intensified to such a degree that now they plotted a double murder. Their usual attitude to spurn the miraculous in the life and work of Christ is really activated and their determined hostility becomes more fierce.

Signs, wonders, and divers miracles characterized the three and more years of the public ministry of our Lord. In confronting the Jews one day He made mention of a great wonder. He spoke of the origin of their wickedness and malevolence. Said He to them, ''Ye are of your father the devil, and the lusts of your father ye will do'' (John 8:44). After laying this charge against them, He threw out a challenge to them, and demanded, ''Which of you convinceth Me of sin?''

There is nothing more aggravating in a company of persons than one man who assumes a much superior attitude, hypocritically acting as if he were perfect. In contrast to such a one, here is the truly perfect Man, the One who could challenge all others to prove that He was otherwise. Here then is the One "who knew no sin" (2 Corinthians 5:21), "Who did no sin" (1 Peter 2:22), for "in Him is no sin" (1 John 3:5).

While they disdainfully refused to accept the challenge, the arrogance and the antipathy of the Jews was further intensified. The very fact that this challenge remains uncontested unto this very day verifies the claims of Christ to sinlessness and the assertions of the Holy Scriptures that the Lord Jesus Christ was "holy, harmless, undefiled, separate from sinners" (Hebrews 7:26). Surely, surely the Lord Himself is the greatest miracle of all time.

He who was pure and holy could touch even a poor leper and heal him without suffering any contamination. The Lord, after healing the unfortunate man, instructed him to go to the priest, perhaps the same priest who had pronounced him unclean and expelled him from among the people. He was there to comply with the law in order that he be restored to his family and to society (Matthew 8:3-4).

The sympathy of the Lord reached out to the handicapped. He restored and gave sight to the blind (Mark 10:46-52), He healed the chronic invalid when all else had failed (John 5:1-16).

To state how many actual resurrections were performed by the Lord during His early sojourn would be presumptive. We know of the widow's son of Nain (Luke 7:11-16). He likewise raised the daughter of the ruler of the synagogue (Matthew 9:18-26; Luke 8:49-56). Reference has already been made to the resurrection of Lazarus. The wonder of such a miracle is certainly impressed upon the sincere and serious thinker (John 11:38-44). There are remarkable proofs here which one cannot honestly discard.

The Apostle Paul, in his introduction to the Epistle to the Romans, gives what might be called a word portrait of Christ, this portrait revealing both His humanity and deity: "His Son Jesus Christ our Lord, which was made of the seed of David according to the flesh; and declared to be the Son of God with power, according to the spirit of holiness, by the resurrection from the dead" (Romans 1:3-4). Vincent comments:

> Though the resurrection is here presented as actually realized in one individual only, the phrase, as everywhere in the New Testament, signifies the resurrection of the dead absolutely and generically—of all the dead, as exemplified, included, and involved in the resurrection of Christ.[1]

All these miracles and many more, with the exception of the Lord's resurrection, were performed in public. These were in nowise as the hidden mysteries, the occult secrets of pagan religions. They were public demonstrations of the Lord's divine nature and power. Manifestly there was a deliberate rejection of obvious facts on the part of the Jewish nation. This resistence of the people to the truth is expressed in Peter's postpentecostal address: "Ye denied the Holy One and the Just, and desired a murderer to be granted unto you; and killed the Prince of life, whom God hath raised from the dead; whereof we are witnesses" (Acts 3:14-15).

Here we bow in adoration, worship, and wonder in the presence of that blessed One, the Seed of David as to His humanity, the Son of God as to His deity. On our part there should be a ready acknowledgment that we cannot understand the hypostatic union of the two natures in Christ; the finite cannot possibly understand the infinite. Faith gladly accepts the truth and in reverence and love pours out the homage of the heart before the Lord Jesus Christ.

---

[1]M. R. Vincent. *Word Studies in the New Testament,* page 664.

5

CHRIST THE ETERNAL SON

One need not be surprised that unbelievers discredit the eternal Sonship of Christ. This phase of the doctrine of Christ is denied by liberal theologians as well as by the heretical cults. Without doubt there may be some ill-informed Christians who do not understand what is meant by Christ's eternal Sonship, but it is regrettable that there is a group, although a minority group, who affirm that they belong to the Lord, who also discredit this doctrine. We must therefore search the Scriptures to ascertain the truth.

There have been two specific errors regarding the eternal Sonship of Christ which have harassed the Church. The first contends that in His humiliation Christ was not conscious of His divine Sonship until after His baptism; the second, that on the cross He lost the consciousness of His Sonship with the Father and that is what intensified His suffering.

Let us examine the Holy Scriptures in an inductive manner. We mean by this that, since God as Father has performed certain acts in, with, or by His Son, we must assume that at such times Christ bore to the Father the relationship of Son.

His Sonship in the premundane past. "Blessed be the God and Father of our Lord Jesus Christ, who hath blessed us with all spiritual blessings in heavenly places in Christ: according as He hath chosen us in Him before the foundation of the world" (Ephesians 1:3-4).

The two verbs "choose" and "bless" are both in the same

tense, the past. God the Father blessed us before the foundation of the world. If He did so as Father, the Father of our Lord Jesus, then at that time the Lord Jesus must have been His Son. The eternal Father, to be such, must of necessity have an eternal Son. The same conclusion is obvious in John 17:24.

His Sonship at creation. "God, who at sundry times and in divers manners spake in time past unto the fathers by the prophets, hath in these last days spoken unto us by His Son [in a Son], whom He hath appointed heir of all things, by whom also He made the worlds [ages]" (Hebrews 1:1-2). In this text we have Christ spoken of as a Son in three tenses of time: first, "Hath in these last days spoken unto us by His Son." This final message from God is in a Son, not through a prophet. This of course refers to the present. In the second place, "Whom [the Son] He hath appointed heir of all things." Here the reference is to the future. Ultimately we read, "By whom [again the Son] He made the worlds." Obviously God in the past programmed the ages. The Son through whom God speaks today is the Son who shall be heir of all things because as the Son He created all things.

His Sonship in preincarnate times. "God sending His own Son in the likeness of sinful flesh, and for sin, condemned sin in the flesh" (Romans 8:3). If Christ were a Son at the time He was sent, He must have been a Son before He actually came.

His Sonship at the incarnation. Prophetically in connection with the birth of our Lord, Isaiah says, "Unto us a child is born, unto us a son is given" (Isaiah 9:6). In the particular verse through which so many have been brought to know the Lord, we read, "For God so loved the world, that He gave His only begotten Son, that whosoever believeth in Him should not perish, but have everlasting life" (John 3:16). We have another a priori argument that indicates that Christ was Son before His incarnation: "God sent His only begotten Son into the world, that we might live through Him" (1 John 4:9).

His Sonship during His public service among His own. Peter proposed to the Lord that he might walk upon the water, but became distracted by the waves and the wind, and cried, "Lord save me." The Lord not only saved Peter but He stilled the storm. "Then they that were in the ship came and worshipped Him, saying, Of a truth Thou art the Son of God" (Matthew 14:28-33).

His Sonship at the crucifixion. "He that spared not His own Son, but delivered Him up for us all, how shall He not with Him also freely give us all things?" (Romans 8:32)

His Sonship in resurrection. "Thou art My Son; this day have I begotten Thee" (Psalm 2:7). This quotation from one of those beautiful Hebrew poems we name the Psalms is applied to Christ when He became the first begotten from among the dead (Hebrews 1:5; Colossians 1:18). This salutation from the Father to the Son is a full acknowledgment of the relationship that had always existed between them. It was an announcement of the accomplishment of Christ in His death and resurrection. This is seen clearly in Acts 13:33. He who was sacrificed as God's own Son was raised from among the dead as the Son of God.

His Sonship throughout eternity. To prove this, only one short quotation from Scripture is necessary: "But unto the Son He saith, Thy throne, O God, is for ever and ever" (Hebrews 1:8).

There was much that our Lord renounced when He came forth in lowly guise to be the Saviour of the world. It is true that He humbled Himself and made Himself of no reputation (Philippians 2:5-11). Here the marginal reading of the King James Version avers, "He emptied Himself," but it does not say of what He emptied Himself. Theologians of different persuasions have propounded what they think this passage means. Many, unfortunately too many, teach that He emptied Himself of His deity and became only a man, a very good man. Others do not go to this extent; they assume that He emptied Himself of His divine attributes. One wonders at such foolishness. How could God empty Himself of His being God and yet remain an entity?

How could one dispossess himself of inherited natural abilities? For example, if one possesses talents in music, can he rid himself of these? Can he possibly will that they cease to exist in him? If this is impossible, how much less could the Lord Jesus in His gracious incarnation dismiss, even on a temporary basis, His divine attributes? He may not use them; He may see fit to veil them. But did He do so fully?

Even this cursory survey of what the Scriptures have to say relative to this important subject reveals that at no time did the Lord Jesus renounce His eternal, intimate relationship with the Father; at no time did He lose the consciousness of His eternal Sonship.

In His prayer in the upper room, on the night He was betrayed, the Lord intimated of what it was that He emptied Himself: "O Father, glorify Thou Me with Thine own self with the glory which I had with Thee before the world was" (John 17:5). Here the Lord refers not only to His preexistence but also to His preincarnate glory with the Father. Does He here imply that which He had once left is to be restored, "glory with the Father"?

All that is involved in this glory is not known; nevertheless there was the worship of the seraphim, the attention of the cherubim, and the constant service of the angels. All these He relinquished, and being found in the fashion of a man, He humbled Himself and became obedient unto death, even the death of a cross. He relinquished only the insignia of His Godhead.

The Lord did not divest Himself of either His essential

nature or His personal attributes. While here on earth He was omnipresent: when Philip brought Nathanael to the Lord Jesus, the Lord said, "An Israelite indeed, in whom there is no guile! . . . Nathanael saith unto Him, Whence knowest Thou me?" The answer of the Lord is indicative of His omnipresence: "Before that Philip called thee, when thou wast under the fig tree, I saw thee." No one can hide from God. Well might Nathanael exclaim, "Rabbi, Thou art the Son of God; Thou art the King of Israel" (John 1:47-49).

When the tax collector at Capernaum questioned Peter as to whether or not His Master paid tribute, he answered in the affirmative but actually was not sure, so he determined to inquire of the Lord. Before he had an opportunity to do so the Lord Jesus prevented (anticipated) him and explained how He was exempt from that particular tax. He then added, "Lest we should offend them, go thou to the sea, and cast an hook, and take up the fish that first cometh up; and when thou hast opened his mouth, thou shalt find a piece of money: that take, and give unto them for Me and thee" (Matthew 17:24-27). This particular incident reveals both the omnipresence and the omniscience of the Lord.

By His omnipresence the Lord Jesus, according to His promise, was always with the apostles, and will always be with those who continue their unfinished ministry. Christ said, "Go ye therefore, and teach all nations . . . and, lo, I am with you alway, even unto the end of the world. Amen" (Matthew 28:19-20).

Peter by the sea of Tiberias certainly attributed omniscience to Christ when he said, "Lord, Thou knowest all things; Thou knowest that I love Thee" (John 21:17). The Apostle John asserts, "Jesus knew from the beginning who they were that believe not, and who should betray Him" (John 6:64). It is also recorded, "Jesus did not commit Himself unto them, because He knew all men, and needed not that any should testify of man; for He knew what was in man'' (John 2:24-25).

There are two related concepts expressed by the word omnipotence: power and authority. These are involved in the statement of Christ as He appeared to the eleven after His resurrection, ''All power is given unto Me in heaven and in earth'' (Matthew 28:18). Omnipotence was certainly in evidence when Christ arose during the storm and said unto the sea, ''Peace, be still. And the wind ceased, and there was a great calm'' (Mark 4:39).

Immutability is another of the attributes of God. Deity alone is unchangeable. The Old Testament records the assertions of God relative to His unchangeableness: ''I am the Lord, I change not'' (Malachi 3:6). This same quality of immutability is attributed to Christ by the writer of the Epistle to the Hebrews. First, this writer applies the words of Psalm 102:25-27, to the Lord Jesus, ''Thou art the same, and Thy years shall have no end'' (Hebrews 1:12). In the second place, he declares, ''Jesus Christ the same yesterday, and to day, and for ever'' (Hebrews 13:8).

These scriptural quotations sufficiently prove the contention that Christ displayed the attributes of God while here on earth, that is, His personal attributes. A study of His moral attributes would result in the very same conclusion.

The Incarnation

The more we contemplate the mystery of Christ (Colossians 2:2), the more are we amazed by the details of His incarnation. Dr. Norman Anderson says of this word, as applied to the Lord Jesus:

> I believe it expresses, better than any other term, the fact that we are here face to face with a subject which, by its very nature, the human mind can never fathom.[1]

---

[1]Norman Anderson, *The Mystery of the Incarnation,* page vi.

The acceptance of the doctrine of the virgin birth of Christ contributes much to our appreciation of the incarnation. James S. Stewart has made a significant statement in his foreword to *The Christ of the Earliest Christians* by William M. Ramsay:

> What we Christians worship is not a human life climbed up to God by a process of deification—it is God coming down into humanity by an act of incarnation, an event of a totally different quality.[1]

We can only concur in the bold assertion of a great theologian, the Apostle Paul, "Without controversy great is the mystery of godliness: God was manifest in the flesh" (1 Timothy 3:16).

The incarnation may be examined from different perspectives. One of much interest is its fulfillment of numerous Old Testament prophecies.

1. *His immaculate conception by Mary through the divine Spirit was plainly predicted.* "A virgin shall conceive, and bear a son, and shall call His name Immanuel" (Isaiah 7:14). Joseph, Mary's espoused husband was told by the angel that the birth of Jesus would be a fulfillment of this prophecy (Matthew 1:19-24).

The details given in Isaiah 7 are understood only through the principle of prophetic interpretation recognized as "partial and complete fulfillment." The birth by the prophetess of Maher-shalal-hash-baz, recorded in Isaiah 8, is the partial fulfillment of the prediction, but Maher-shalal-hash-baz certainly was not Immanuel, God with us. For the complete fulfillment of this prophecy the world had to wait several centuries, until the birth of Christ, when He came as Immanuel.

2. *The place of the Saviour's birth was foretold.* "Thou Bethlehem Ephratah, though thou be little among the thousands of Judah, yet out of thee shall He come forth unto Me

[1]William M. Ramsay, *The Christ of the Earliest Christians*, page 10.

that is to be ruler in Israel; whose goings forth have been from of old, from everlasting'' (Micah 5:2). The chief priests and the scribes knew this passage and did not hesitate to apply it to their Messiah, when interrogated by Herod (Matthew 2:1-6; Luke 2:4-7), but they failed to relate it to the child of Mary, although cruel Herod did: ''Then Herod, when he had privily called the wise men, enquired of them diligently what time the star appeared. And he sent them to Bethlehem, and said, Go and search diligently for the young child; and when ye have found Him, bring me word again, that I may come and worship Him also. . . . Then Herod, when he saw that he was mocked of the wise men, was exceeding wroth, and sent forth, and slew all the children that were in Bethlehem, and in all the coasts thereof, from two years old and under, according to the time which he had diligently enquired of the wise men'' (Matthew 2:7-8,16).

3. *The ministry of Christ was also predicted.* This has been well recorded by the Prophet Isaiah: ''The Spirit of the Lord GOD is upon Me; because the LORD hath anointed Me to preach good tidings unto the meek; He hath sent Me to bind up the brokenhearted, to proclaim liberty to the captives, and the opening of the prison to them that be bound; to proclaim the acceptable year of the LORD'' (Isaiah 61:1-2a). In the synagogue at Nazareth, where Jesus had been brought up, He publicly read this passage and boldly asserted, ''This day is this Scripture fulfilled in your ears'' (Luke 4:16-22).

4. *The injustice suffered by our Lord before Pilate and Herod was foretold by Isaiah.* ''He was taken from prison and from judgment'' (Isaiah 53:8). Difficult to understand as these words may be, it is generally conceded that they indicate the Lord Jesus did not restrain His persecutors by His divine power; consequently He was given over to a cruel death in violation of every principle of justice. ''Pilate, when he had called together the chief priests and the rulers and the

people, said unto them, Ye have brought this man unto me, as one that perverteth the people: and, behold, I, having examined Him before you, have found no fault in this man touching those things whereof ye accuse Him. . . . They were instant with loud voices, requiring that He might be crucified. And the voices of them and of the chief priests prevailed. And Pilate gave sentence that it should be as they required'' (Luke 23:1-13).

5. *The crucifixion of Christ was described in Psalm 22 centuries before it took place.* Crucifixion was a most brutal means of execution. Numbers of the ancient nations and empires practiced it—the Assyrians, the Egyptians, and, of course, the Romans. There were two modes of crucifixion, one was to bind the victim with thongs to a cross or a pole and leave him there to be devoured by wild beasts and birds of prey—a slow agonizing death. The second mode was to nail the victim to the gibbet through the hands and feet. Although a quicker death it too would be most excruciating.

The Romans reserved this type of execution for slaves and vicious criminals. No Roman citizen could be crucified legally. Our blessed, impeccable, holy Lord Jesus was nailed to the cross as a criminal. That Israel's Messiah should have thus died is most remarkable, for stoning was the Jewish means of capital punishment. Indubitably this had been predetermined by God.

There is no doubt as to how Christ was executed; it was by means of nails. Prophetically the Psalmist in his delineation of our Saviour's crucifixion writes, ''They pierced My hands and My feet'' (Psalm 22:16). Isaiah says, ''He was wounded [pierced through] for our transgressions, He was bruised [crushed] for our iniquities'' (Isaiah 53:5).

The disciples knew that the Lord Jesus had been nailed to the cross. Thomas said, ''Except I . . . see in His hands the print of the nails, and . . . thrust my hand into His side, I will not believe'' (John 20:25). To him the Lord said, ''Thomas, reach hither thy finger, and behold My hands, and reach hither thy hand, and thrust it into My side: and be not faithless, but believing'' (John 20:27). The mode of our Lord's cruel sufferings is clearly indicated.

In a future day when repentant Israel has been fully recovered and basks in the glory of her enthroned Messiah, the King of kings and the Lord of lords, ''They shall look upon Me,'' Messiah shall say, ''whom they have pierced, and they shall mourn'' (Zechariah 12:10). Yes, the contrite nation shall regret and lament over their malicious and nefarious deed.

Perhaps this should be added: scourging was part of the whole procedure of execution, but the mockery, the taunting, and the piercing of our Lord's side were simply evidence of human hatred and brutality.

6. *Even the burial of Jesus was foretold in the prophecy of Isaiah.* ''He made [appointed] His grave with the wicked, and with the rich in His death'' (Isaiah 53:9).

It was Roman law that the bodies of the crucified remain upon the crosses. An exemption to this was conceded to the Jews. The body of a Jewish criminal could be removed and buried at the scene of execution. Such a grave was prepared for the Lord Jesus, but God had predetermined that it should be otherwise.

The historical account of His burial reads, ''When the even was come, there came a rich man of Arimathea, named Joseph. . . . He went to Pilate, and begged the body of Jesus. . . . When Joseph had taken the body, he wrapped it in a clean linen cloth, and laid it in his own new tomb, which he had hewn out in the rock'' (Matthew 27:57-60). Other details are added in the accounts of His burial given in the other Gospels. ''He who was crucified as a felon was buried as a king,'' laid to rest in a rich man's sepulcher.

The Old Testament predictions which were fulfilled through the incarnation of the Lord Jesus provide another proof of the veracity and the inspiration of the sacred Scriptures.

At Bethlehem the preincarnate Son of God clothed Himself with humanity.

> Here is to be introduced His various sonships—the title Son of God suggesting the divine; Son of Man, the racial; Son of Mary, the human; Son of David, the Messianic and Jewish; Son of Abraham, the redemptive.[1]

[1]Lewis Sperry Chafer, *Systematic Theology*, volume VII, page 79.

6

THE ATONEMENT

Through constant use the word *atonement* has come to stand for the whole work of Christ in His death at Calvary and its results. Actually it presents an Old Testament concept, that of covering over sin in order to maintain a proper relationship with God. The word itself occurs only once in the New Testament (Romans 5:11) where it would be more correctly rendered *reconciliation,* as is shown in the marginal reading.

The general understanding of the word today is that it expresses the particular results of the death, the sacrifice of Christ in making possible the reconciliation of man with God.

Any apprehension of substitutionary atonement must take into consideration the character of God, the predicament of man through sin, the voluntary offering of Christ, and the blessed consequences of the Lord's accomplishments at Calvary. In other words, one must observe carefully the necessity of sacrificial atonement, the value of the offering of Himself, and the results of that immolation.

The Character of God

The Bible in itself is not an apologetic, it does not prove the existence of God. It assumes that all who read it believe in the eternal, infinite, supreme Spirit (John 4:24). The Bible opens with the bold assertion, "In the beginning God created the heaven and the earth'' (Genesis 1:1), and it contains such indubitable statements as, ''The eternal God is thy refuge, and underneath are the everlasting arms'' (Deuteronomy 33:27).

The Prophet Isaiah throws out the challenge: ''Hast thou not known? hast thou not heard, that the everlasting God, the LORD, the Creator of the ends of the earth, fainteth not, neither is weary? There is no searching of His understanding'' (Isaiah 40:28). A song for the sons of Korah intoned the stanza, ''Thy throne, O God, is for ever and ever: the sceptre of Thy Kingdom is a right sceptre'' (Psalm 45:6).

Not only does the Bible reveal evidence of the divine personal attributes of God: His omnipotence, omniscience, omnipresence, immutability, and eternality, but it describes the perfect moral attributes of God. A certain appreciation of these is necessary to an understanding of the true character of God.

1. *''God is love,''* avers the Apostle John (1 John 4:8). Love therefore is a characteristic of His very nature; consequently it is natural for God to love spontaneously and ideally. The love of God to man is the basis of His self-revelation. Love at the beginning was the reason for God's communicating with Adam.

It has been well said that love is God's desire to impart Himself and every good to other persons, and to possess them for His own. Love has been defined as the will to exercise its powers, to possess its object, and to enrich that object throughout its whole existence. How true this is of the love of God. The love of God for man is the cause of every temporal blessing. In providence ''He maketh His sun to rise on the evil and on the good, and sendeth rain on the just and on the unjust'' (Matthew 5:45).

The love of God is also the origin of every spiritual blessing for the believer: ''Blessed be the God and Father of our Lord

Jesus Christ, who hath blessed us with all spiritual blessings in heavenly places in Christ'' (Ephesians 1:3).

The love of God is the power behind the sufferings and the sacrifice of Christ:

> ''For God so loved the world, that He gave His only begotten Son'' (John 3:16): What proclamation of the gospel has been so oft on the lips of missionaries and preachers in every age since it was first uttered? What has sent such thrilling sensation through millions of mankind? What has been honored to bring such multitudes to the feet of Christ? What to kindle in the cold selfish breasts of mortals the fires of self-sacrificing love to mankind, as these words of transparent simplicity, yet overpowering majesty?[1]

Furthermore, ''He [God] spared not His own Son, but delivered Him up for us all'' (Romans 8:32). How little do we understand what it cost God to hand over His beloved Son to the suffering of sin and the penalty of sin, as well as to maltreatment of wicked and depraved men who were energized by Satan.

2. The same Apostle John acknowledged that ''*God is light*'' (1 John 1:5). As light is white, pure, and transparent, and is the revealer of what is hidden and defiled, even so is infinite holiness: ''O LORD . . . glorious in holiness'' (Exodus 15:11). Holiness is more than a denunciation of moral evil; it is the positive affirmation of purity itself.

The Prophet Isaiah and one of the psalmists join to make a declaration of God's holiness: ''Holy, holy, holy, is the LORD of hosts: the whole earth is full of His glory'' (Isaiah 6:3). ''Exalt ye the Lord our God . . . for He is holy'' (Psalm 99:5-9). The Apostle Peter applies a quotation from Leviticus 11:43-45 to all New Testament believers: ''As He which hath called you is holy, so be ye holy in all manner of conversation [in every mode of living]; because it is written, Be ye holy; for I am holy'' (1 Peter 1:15-16).

---

[1]Jamieson, Fausset, and Brown, *Commentary, New Testament,* page 132.

A preacher of an old school used to say, "God was so holy that He could not pass over sin with the slightest degree of allowance." Many, like Israel, "being ignorant of God's righteousness [holiness] . . . have not submitted themselves unto the righteousness of God" (Romans 10:3). They are in a state of darkness and defilement, avoiding the rays of infinite light.

The Predicament of Man

Man, when created by God, was in a state of innocence. He enjoyed the love of God, and stood in the presence of divine holiness without fear. Through the fall man was expelled from the holy presence of God, albeit he was never excluded from the love of God.

The fall. In spite of the claims of moral evolution it is obvious that man is not what he was when first created. There has not been any cultural and intellectual development; much rather there has been a constant decadence.

Man was created in the image and likeness of God, a perfect and a rational being. He was capable of using his own will freely, and when tried by sin, this he did. Eve was a companion made by God and thoroughly suitable to Adam in his aloneness.

God had entrusted man as to life, its purpose, occupation, and maintenance: "Be fruitful, and multiply, and replenish the earth, and subdue it: and have dominion over the fish of the sea, and over the fowl of the air, and over every living thing that moveth upon the earth" (Genesis 1:28). God also cautioned Adam saying, "Of every tree of the garden thou mayest freely eat: but of the tree of the knowledge of good and evil, thou shalt not eat of it: for in the day thou eatest thereof thou shalt surely die" (Genesis 2:16-17).

While there is not prehistoric man, there may have been prehistoric animals. If so, these had disappeared before Adam's time. Death was no meaningless intimidation. Adam must have known what death was. He had probably seen its evidence in the giant animals of pre-Eden periods.

Satan brought about the fall of man by means of what has been called the avenue of moral action. This road of moral action has been delineated by the Apostle John: "The lust of the flesh, and the lust of the eyes, and the pride of life" (1 John 2:16).

When Eve, under the deceptive influence of Satan, saw that the tree was good for food (the lust of the flesh), and pleasant to the eyes (the lust of the eyes), and a tree to be desired to make one wise (the pride of life), "she took of the fruit thereof, and did eat, and gave also unto her husband with her; and he did eat. And the eyes of them both were opened, and they knew that they were naked; and they sewed fig leaves together, and made themselves aprons" (Genesis 3:6-7).

> The history of every temptation, and of every sin, is the same, the outward object of attraction—the inward commotion of mind—the increase and triumph of passionate desire, ending in the degradation, slavery, and ruin of the soul.
>
> Shame, remorse, fear, a sense of guilt, feelings to which they had hitherto been strangers, disordered their minds, and led them to shun Him whose approach they used to welcome.[1]

Human guilt may be considered as the state of having committed an offense against God. This in turn results in an inward conflict of conscience and a self-accusation of misconduct before the Lord, a violation of His law.

A penalty is the punishment of guilt. In the case of man's sin against God, infinite holiness imposes the penalty, which is death. Adam was distinctly told, "In the day that thou eatest thereof [the tree of the knowledge of good and evil] thou shalt surely die" (Genesis 2:17). The process of death

---

[1]Jamieson, Fausset, and Brown, *Commentary, Old Testament,* page 19.

began immediately. Another rendering of verse 17 reads, "In dying thou shalt die." Man must be prepared from birth to die. The full penalty of sin is death in all its aspects—spiritual, physical, and eternal (the second death, Revelation 20:14).

While love may mourn the sin of humanity, holiness demands that it be punished.

Lessons from the Old Testament

While the Levitical economy is a puzzle to many unbelievers, and has been a hindrance to belief in the Bible in a few cases, nevertheless it has illuminated the minds of hundreds; through it they have understood the way of salvation.

Human impotency. The whole course of history reveals how impossible it is for man to extricate himself from the condition of death into which sin brought him. He is dead in sins (Ephesians 2:1). He is distant from God (Ephesians 2:12-13). He is blinded by Satan (2 Corinthians 4:4). He is in himself without strength (Romans 5:6).

If man therefore is to be delivered from the power and the penalty of his sin, this must be accomplished by means and instrumentalities apart from himself altogether. These means must be capable of reaching him in his need and depravity.

The Levitical ritualism. The entire Levitical order was devised by God to teach, not only Israel but all others, three basic principles. First, "The soul that sinneth, it shall die" (Ezekiel 18:4; Leviticus 22:9; 24:15-16). Secondly, this penalty could be endured vicariously; the offender could offer in death a perfect animal from his flock (Leviticus 4:27-35). Thirdly, only when a satisfactory substitute had been offered could there be forgiveness of sin (Leviticus 4:31-35).

While holiness sentenced and executed the guilty, love provided a means of forgiveness and acceptance with God through a vicarious atonement.

The Person of Christ

In order to redeem mankind from sin and death, God has united in one glorious personality—Jesus Christ the Lord—both natures, the human and the divine. This glorious personality was sent in order to reveal God to man and to reconcile man to God. This work of revealing God to man and reconciling man to God was accomplished by Christ in His life and death.

There are several names and titles which belong to the Lord by virtue of His manhood. He was known as "the son of Mary" (Mark 6:3). He was given the name Jesus, the Greek equivalent of Joshua, meaning Saviour (Matthew 1:21). He called Himself "the Son of man." Christ used this title during His public ministry more frequently than any other (Matthew 20:28). He was acknowledged by His disciples as "the Christ," the Messiah (Matthew 16:13-16). By Herod He was considered "the King of the Jews" (Matthew 2:2).

Certain statements are made concerning the Lord in His earthly life as He witnessed the ravages of sin, and as He experienced the effect of that sin in personal sufferings.

Christ's sufferings in the flesh were real. Isaiah states that as Jehovah's Perfect Servant Christ was "a man of sorrows, and acquainted with grief." He then adds, "Surely He hath borne our griefs, and carried our sorrows: yet we did esteem Him stricken, smitten of God, and afflicted" (Isaiah 53:4).

The Spirit of God applies these words to the life and ministry of our Lord: "And when Jesus was come into Peter's house, He saw his wife's mother laid, and sick of a fever. And He touched her hand, and the fever left her: and she arose, and ministered unto them. When the even was come, they brought unto Him many that were possessed with devils: and He cast out the spirits with His word, and healed all that were sick: That it might be fulfilled which was spoken by Esaias the prophet, saying, Himself took our infirmities, and bare our sicknesses'' (Matthew 8:14-17).

Christ was touched with the feeling of human infirmity.

Christ's sufferings in life were exemplary. Peter declares that ''Christ also suffered for us, leaving us an example, that ye should follow His steps'' (1 Peter 2:21-25). It is interesting to note how closely the vicarious sufferings of Christ are related to His exemplary sufferings: ''Christ also suffered for us, leaving us an example, that ye should follow His steps: Who did no sin, neither was guile found in His mouth: Who, when He was reviled, reviled not again; when He suffered, He threatened not; but committed Himself to Him that judgeth righteously: Who His own self bare our sins in His own body on the tree'' (1 Peter 2:21-24). Obviously the Spirit of God teaches that apart from the acceptance of the former, it is impossible that we adequately follow the latter.

The sufferings of Christ in Gethsemane were anticipatory. ''Being in an agony He prayed more earnestly: and His sweat was as it were great drops of blood falling down to the ground'' (Luke 22:44).

F. J. Huegel, in his volume, *The Cross of Christ, The Throne of God,* writes:

> Jesus Himself, as to His humanity, at one time was, it seems, at the point of shrinking: ''Father, if it be possible, let this cup pass.'' It was in the garden. He had not yet come to the real thing. Even the shadow made Him sweat blood. ''Surely, Father, there must be some other way of saving a lost world. They have the sermon on the Mount. Father . . . I have lived a perfect life before them . . . they have My example . . . Why. . . .'' Ah, but He does not shrink. ''Not My will but Thine be done,'' He cries, and He goes forth from His holy seculsion.[1]

Even Huegel with his vivid imagination does not attempt to describe ''the cup.'' Whoever could? What does man

---

[1]F. J. Huegel, *The Cross of Christ, and the Throne of God,* page 49.

know, even redeemed man, of the component parts of that dreadful cup?

Was the Lord Jesus afraid to die? Was He more timid than many others have been? Was it the expectation of even the death of the cross with its excruciating pain and agony alone that caused His sweat like drops of blood to drip upon the earth?

No, He was not afraid to die, if death only was involved in that experience. Sin, the guilt of humanity, and the penalty of sin, the punishment demanded by infinite holiness, met upon one person, the God-Man, as Christ hung nailed to the cross. Add to these the major component of that potion, divine abandonment. Our beloved Lord, knowing the entire bitter content, said, "The cup which My Father hath given Me, shall I not drink it?" Here in wonderment we worship!

The sufferings of Christ on the cross were expiratory. "For He hath made Him to be sin for us, who knew no sin; that we might be made the righteousness of God in Him" (2 Corinthians 4:21). "For Christ also hath once suffered for sins, the just for the unjust, that He might bring us to God, being put to death in the flesh, but quickened by the Spirit" (1 Peter 3:18).

Types and Shadows

A Biblical type is an Old Testament picture, pattern, or model of a New Testament reality.

In the Levitical economy there are many types of Christ; these are seen in persons, events, ceremonies, and offerings. The offerings of the Old Testament were foreshadowings of the sacrifice of the Lord Jesus upon the cross. We shall center our attention on the five major offerings presented in the early chapters of the book of Leviticus, for they typify different aspects of the sacrifice of the Lord Jesus.

The burnt offering was a sweet savor offering; the entire animal was consumed upon the brazen altar. It typified Christ's voluntary death as it delighted the heart of His Father God. His was perfect obedience to the will of God (Hebrews 9:14; Philippians 2:8).

The meal or cereal offering accompanied the burnt offering. It was composed of fine flour, oil, frankincense, and salt. A handful was placed upon the altar, and the larger portion, that which remained, was food for Israel's priest. It typified the perfect sinless life of the Lord Jesus. The entire life of the Lord was well pleasing to the Father (Luke 3:22).

The peace offering was an animal, part of which, the inwards and the fat, was consumed upon the brazen altar while the breast and the shoulders were for the priests. This offering typifies Christ in His death as bringing God and man together. God and the believer both alike find pleasure in the peace offering of the Saviour; they enjoy reconciliation and fellowship (Ephesians 2:13-18).

It should be understood that in the sweet savor offerings, the saint is seen identified with Christ in His acceptance before God (Ephesians 1:6). In the nonsweet savor offerings the sinner is seen identified with Christ under the judgment of God.

The sin offering was also an animal. It was wholly burnt, not upon the brazen altar but, to indicate God's abhorrence of sin, outside the camp.

In the Hebrew the same word represents both "sin" and "sin offering." Here Christ is typified as forsaken of God and paying the full penalty of sin (Hebrews 13:11-15; Romans 8:2). God in Christ judged sin, the evil principle that man inherits.

The trespass offering was in like manner an animal offered for single and personal offenses. It typified the Lord Jesus making atonement for the sinful acts of man, and restoring to

God that of which man had deprived Him. In certain cases the sacrifice to God had to be supplemented by a restitution for the loss incurred by the offense. Prophetically it was said of the Lord, He restored that which He took not away (Psalm 69:4).

In History

During the years of His ministry the Lord on several occasions intimated that He would give His life sacrificially. He spoke clearly of His death to His disciples but they did not understand Him (Luke 18:31-34). He spoke pictorially of His death as the Good Shepherd in a public discourse (John 10:14-15). He intimated His death symbolically in the upper room when He instituted the Lord's Supper on the night of His betrayal (Mark 14:22-25).

Literally the sacrificial death of Christ is recorded by Luke the historian as an act of premeditated murder. He cites Peter's words to the Jewish people who gathered because of the healing of the lame man at the entrance into the temple: "Ye denied the Holy One and the Just, and desired a murderer to be granted unto you; and killed the Prince of life, whom God hath raised from the dead; whereof we are witnesses" (Acts 3:14-15). Similar strong language is used by Luke in chapters 5 and 7.

This act was accomplished by crucifixion. "When they were come to the place, which is called Calvary, there they crucified Him" (Luke 23:33). And that death was properly certified by the Roman governor, Pilate: "Pilate marvelled if He were already dead: and calling unto him the centurion, he asked him whether He had been any while dead. And when he knew it of the centurion, he gave the body to Joseph" (Mark 15:44-45).

Joseph of Arimathaea and Nicodemus, who had come to Jesus one night, "took the body of Jesus, and wound it in linen clothes with the spices, as the manner of the Jews is to bury. Now in the place where He was crucified there was a garden; and in the garden a new sepulchre, wherein was never man yet laid. There laid they Jesus therefore because of the Jews' preparation day'' (John 19:40-42).

Crucifixion usually was performed in some secluded spot outside the city, for generally the bodies were left until devoured by beasts and birds. Under Rome burial was generally forbidden, except in the case of the Jews, when an exception was decreed in their favor.

This agonizing mode of death was reserved for slaves, malefactors, and traitors. In ancient Rome exemption from it was one of the privileges of Roman citizenship.

Christ was not a slave; it was well known that He was not a malefactor; consequently, the Jews pressed the accusation of sedition. This made Him a traitor to Rome. By this means they accomplished His death.

In Doctrine

The doctrine of the sacrificial death of the Lord Jesus is very comprehensive and leads also into a study of the different effects of His sacrifice upon man and upon creation. It will be necessary that certain terms be used and explained.

The sacrifice of Christ was substitutionary. The death of Christ was vicarious for He became the substitute of all who receive Him. Each believer can say, ''The Son of God . . . loved me, and gave Himself for me'' (Galatians 2:20). The Apostle Peter makes an explicit and forceful statement in this same regard: ''Christ also hath once suffered for sins [propitiation], the just for the unjust [substitution], that He might bring us to God [reconciliation], being put to death in the flesh, but quickened by the Spirit'' (1 Peter 3:18).

This substitutionary aspect of the death of Christ is considered by some to be an ethical sacrifice, in that it accomplished for man before God what man could not do for himself. It thus satisfies the righteous claims of infinite holiness against man.

Guillebaud in his excellent book, *Why the Cross?* says:

> Instead of a judge punishing an innocent party in the place of the criminal, we have a Triune Judge. One of whose persons identifies Himself with the nature of the criminal in all except his sin, then takes the sin itself upon Him, and suffers the penalty of His own law which indeed has no existence independent of Him. Moreover, not only is there this identity between the substitute and the Judge, but also in a mysterious sense between the Substitute and the criminal, when the latter becomes willing to accept the identification.[1]

The sacrifice of Christ was propitiatory. The word satisfaction is frequently used as a synonym for propitiation because the sacrifice of Christ rendered satisfaction to God for the affront and the loss God sustained through the fall of man. The sacrifice of Christ was not offered in order to incline God to love man; this He always did. It was offered in one of its aspects to satisfy and meet the claims of divine justice. The wonders of this sacrifice lie in the fact that by this means God met His own demands, satisfying His own righteousness, and appeasing His wrath against sin; for this is in evidence although He loves the sinner. The sacrifice of Christ may be viewed as God's self-propitiation. The Apostle Paul, in dealing with the great subject of the justification of the believer, says that this is accomplished through the redemption that is in Christ Jesus; "Whom God hath set forth to be a propitiation [a mercy seat]" (Romans 3:24-25).

The Apostle John asserts that Christ "is the propitiation for our sins: and not for ours only, but also for the sins of the whole world" (1 John 2:2).

Divine righteousness demands propitiation for sin. Before

---

[1]H. E. Guillebaud, *Why the Cross?* pages 147-148.

God can manifest Himself in grace, He must receive full satisfaction for the harm and loss occasioned by the fall of man. Christ is that propitiation. He has satisfied the claims of holiness and made it possible to extend mercy to fallen humanity.

The sacrifice of Christ is expiatory. The word expiation is not found in the Scriptures, but the truth expressed by it permeates the whole Christian canon. It intimates that since penalty has been endured, forgiveness ensues. An example of this is given by the writer of the Epistle to the Ephesians as he includes the readers with himself: "In whom we have redemption through His blood, the forgiveness of sins" (Ephesians 1:7). Christ has died, has borne the penalty our sins merited, and through His redemptive work has freed us from the bondage of sin; now we receive the forgiveness of sins.

During the years of His public ministry, did our Lord have this particular aspect of His sacrifice before Him? He certainly dispensed the forgiveness of sins very graciously and readily. On one occasion when Jesus said to a palsied man, "Son, thy sins be forgiven thee," some scribes found fault. Among themselves they asked the question, "Why doth this man thus speak blasphemies? Who can forgive sins but God only?"

The Lord Jesus knowing that they so reasoned within themselves, said, "Whether is it easier to say to the sick of the palsy, Thy sins be forgiven thee; or to say, Arise, and take up thy bed, and walk? But that ye may know that the Son of man hath power on earth to forgive sins (He saith to the sick of the palsy,) I say unto thee, Arise, and take up thy bed, and go thy way" (Mark 2:5-11).

In this kind act, the Lord gave the spiritual priority over the physical. Inasmuch as God can forgive sins only on the basis of propitiation, it seems evident that the Lord Jesus had this constantly in mind. Expiation is the blessed experience for the believer, but the divine basis is propitiation.

The sacrifice of Christ was redemptive. The doctrine of redemption in the New Testament reveals clearly that Christ by His death on the cross paid the ransom price and thus redeemed the slaves of sin from their condemned position before God.

The result of Christ's redemptive work may be experienced by the believer in the present, and it will be a glorious accomplishment in the future.

The present. There are certain prepositions used in the New Testament related to the idea of redemption. An understanding of these helps to ascertain the fullness of this extensive work of Christ and the resulting benefits.

"With." The preposition "with" and the related "by" indicate the means used to accomplish redemption. The Apostle Peter informs us, "Ye were not redeemed with corruptible things, as silver and gold, from your vain conversation received by tradition from your fathers; but with the precious blood of Christ, as of a lamb without blemish and without spot" (1 Peter 1:18). Here the death of Christ is viewed as the ransom price of the deliverance of the sinner. The Lord Jesus made reference to His death in this same light: "The Son of man came not to be ministered unto, but to minister, and to give His life a ransom for many" (Mark 10:45; Matthew 20:28). The death of Christ is the price paid for the release of the believing sinner.

"From." This preposition means "out of" and intimates the position or the condition from which a believer is delivered by the death of Christ, the ransom paid. The believer is "made free from sin" (Romans 6:18). Furthermore, "Christ hath redeemed us from the curse of the law, being made a curse for us" (Galatians 3:13). He has also redeemed us "from all iniquity, [to] purify unto Himself a peculiar people, zealous of good works" (Titus 2:14). Such then was the marketplace of bondage and slavery where He purchased us for Himself.

"To." This preposition implies that, since the ransom has been paid for the believer's release from the bondage of sin and the curse of a broken law, he has become the property of God.

In the song of the redeemed in the glory all three prepositions appear: "Thou art worthy to take the book, and to open the seals thereof: for Thou wast slain, and hast redeemed us *to* God *by* Thy blood *out of* every kindred, and tongue, and nation; And hast made us unto our God kings and priests: and we shall reign on the earth" (Revelation 5:9-10).

Well might the Apostle Paul remind us, "Ye are bought with a price: therefore glorify God in your body, and in your spirit, which are God's" (1 Corinthians 6:20).

The future. The Apostle Paul instructed the saints at Rome concerning the extent of the glorious liberty of the children of God, that is, in regard to the final results of the ransom paid by Christ at Calvary: "We ourselves groan within ourselves, waiting for the adoption, to wit, the redemption of our body" (Romans 8:23). He also told the Ephesians that they had received the seal of divine possession in view of the future: "Ye were sealed with the Holy Spirit of promise, Which is the earnest of our inheritance until the redemption of the purchased possession, unto the praise of His glory. . . . Ye are sealed unto the day of redemption" (Ephesians 1:13-14, 4:30).

The eternal. The work of redemption by Christ does not only produce emancipation from bondage, but it results in eternal liberty. "By His own blood He [Christ] entered in once into the holy place, having obtained eternal redemption for us" (Hebrews 9:12). The redemption of the believer is not only freedom from the bondage of sin in the present, it is being brought into intimate relationship with God and into the hope of eternal liberty and life.

The sacrifice of Chirst is reconciliatory. In secular affairs reconciliation is an act by which estranged persons are restored to friendship. It is an act by which each becomes ready to receive the other. Divine reconciliation, according to the Scriptures, is the act by which only one party, man—for he alone is estranged—is reconciled to God. The Word of God does not suggest that God become reconciled to man. God is love and is always ready to receive man, who in his sins has estranged himself to God, becoming an enemy toward God: "For . . . when we were enemies, we were reconciled to God by the death of His Son [and] . . . being reconciled, we shall be saved by His life" (Romans 5:10).

Divine reconciliation is presented in Holy Scripture under four aspects:

As a provision. "God was in Christ, reconciling the world unto Himself, not imputing their trespasses unto them; and hath committed unto us the word of reconciliation" (2 Corinthians 5:19). Christ, in His death, by imputation was made sin for us that, by imputation, we might be made the righteousness of God in Him. Consequently we are brought into the new creation in Christ where all things of the old creation in Adam have passed away. The believer is no longer dead in sin; he is alive in Christ. He is no longer at a distance; he has been brought near. He is no longer condemned; he is justified. Truly old things have passed away and all things have become new.

While this provisional aspect of reconciliation is for all mankind, for "God was in Christ, reconciling the world unto Himself," this does not suggest universal salvation, only a universal provision.

As an experience. "We were reconciled to God by the death of His son. . . . And not only so, but we also joy in God through our Lord Jesus Christ, by whom we have now received the atonement [reconciliation]'' (Romans 5:10-11). The verb *to reconcile* used in verse 10 is in the passive voice, which means that man does nothing, but that, through the death of Christ, God does everything for man. Verse 11 intimates that all man does is enjoy the provision God has made for him. Through the marginal reading it will be seen that Paul and the saints at Rome, those included in the pronoun ''we,'' had simply received the reconciliation.

For the races. Paul shows that Christ in His death became ''our peace,'' and that Jews and Gentiles form one body in the Lord: ''For He is our peace, who hath . . . broken down the middle wall of partition between us; Having abolished in His flesh the enmity . . . for to make in Himself of twain one new man, so making peace; and that He might reconcile both [Jew and Gentile] unto God in one body by the cross, having slain the enmity thereby'' (Ephesians 2:14-16).

For the universe. It is necessary to understand that sin originated in the mind and heart of Satan. There are reasons for believing that Isaiah makes reference to this initial act when he laments, ''How art thou fallen from heaven, O Lucifer, son of the morning! how art thou cut down to the ground, which didst weaken the nations! For thou hast said, in thine heart, I will ascend into heaven, I will exalt my throne above the stars of God: I will sit also upon the mount of the congregation, in the sides of the north: I will ascend above the heights of the clouds; I will be like the most High'' (Isaiah 14:12-14).

The reconciliatory work of Christ is seen eventually reaching out beyond man into the material universe. To the Colossians the apostle wrote concerning the extent of the work of the Lord, ''Having made peace through the blood of His cross, by Him to reconcile all things to Himself; by Him, I say, whether they be things in earth or things in heaven'' (Colossians 1:20).

Like redemption, reconciliation will affect the whole groaning creation. By means of reconciliation God will bring the material heaven and earth back into proper and blessed relationship to Himself. When this has been accomplished, "The wilderness and the solitary place shall be glad for them; and the desert shall rejoice, and blossom as the rose" (Isaiah 35:1). The reconciliatory sacrifice of Christ will ultimately result in the restitution of all things. In the meantime, "The heaven must receive [our Lord Jesus] until the times of restitution of all things, which God hath spoken by the mouth of all His holy prophets since the world began" (Acts 3:21).

As a summation of all that has been covered regarding the atoning work of Christ the words of Alan M. Stibbs in his foreword to *Why the Cross?* by Archdeacon Guillebaud will be helpful:

> Thought of His death as His supreme task was clearly present in Christ's own mind from the beginning of His public ministry. In accepting John's baptism He was numbered with the transgressors. He thus identified Himself with sinners, and may well have been consciously consecrating Himself to the work of bearing and washing away our sin. Later, during His ministry, and particularly towards its end, our Lord's mind about it was unmistakable. He regarded it as God ordained: "thus is it written." As James Denney said, "He saw it as the will of God, from that Scripture which was for Him the Word of God." So He accepted it as necessary.[1]

---

[1]H. E. Guillebaud, *Why the Cross?* page vii.

7
CHRIST'S TRIUMPHANT RESURRECTION

Professor Louis Gaussen has left in his writings a great legacy to the Church of Christ. Among his writings is the following paragraph:

> He is risen. Such is the voice of all preceding ages—the voice of the whole Christian people from the days of the apostles—a voice invariably precise, clear, and unhesitating. We have listened to all the traditions of ancient times to ascertain whether one discordant sound might reach us from within the compass of the ancient Church, and we have been able to perceive none.

The resurrection is the greatest miracle of Christ. It is the foundation upon which the entire structure of Christianity is built. The Old Testament illustrates it in the case of Abraham and Isaac: "Abraham . . . accounting that God was able to raise him [Isaac] up, even from the dead; from whence also he received him in a figure" (Genesis 22; Hebrews 11:19). The Lord Jesus Himself predicted it: "The Son of man shall be delivered . . . condemned . . . to death . . . and the third day He shall rise again" (Mark 10:33-34). The angels declared it: "He is not here: for He is risen, as He said. Come, see the place where the Lord lay" (Matthew 28:1-8). The apostles taught it: "He [Paul] preached unto them Jesus, and the resurrection" (Acts 17:18). The Lord Jesus in triumph and glory proclaimed it: "I am the First and the Last, and the Living One: and I became dead, and behold, I am living to the ages of the ages, and have the keys of death and of hades" (Revelation 1:17-18 New Translation).

What a remarkable proof the resurrection is of the deity of our Lord. The Apostle Paul says that He is "declared to be the Son of God with power, according to the spirit of holiness, by the resurrection from the dead" (Romans 1:4). This very important historical event merits a thorough investigation. It should be examined from every possible angle.

A Historical Event

Inasmuch as there are certain heresies which deny the resurrection of Christ it is necessary that we be sure that He actually died.

His death was certified. Pilate doubted that Christ was dead. When Joseph sought the body of Jesus for burial, Pilate was not satisfied until he had ascertained the fact from the centurion who had been in charge of the execution. Only when thus convinced did he release the body of the Lord. The burial of that precious body was directed by the honorable councilor, Joseph of Arimathaea, and he was assisted by the rabbi, Nicodemus. The death of Christ was certified by the representative of the Roman government, Pilate. It was confirmed by soldiers of the Roman army under the centurion, by the Jewish Sanhedrin, by Joseph, and by a representative of the Jew's religion, Nicodemus. No other death was ever so certified and confirmed as that of the Lord Jesus.

The burial of Jesus was foretold by Isaiah some seven hundred years before the Lord was born. Said the prophet, "He made His grave with the wicked, and with the rich in His death; because He had done no violence, neither was any deceit in His mouth" (Isaiah 53:9). This statement has been explained already, but the clause, "With the rich in His death," might be more clearly understood if the apparent affluence of Joseph and Nicodemus is recalled. The fact is, He was buried by a secret disciple, a friend with influence.

His burial was discussed in the Jewish parliament and was

approved by the Roman governor. It was also well known by the temple guards: "The chief priests and Pharisees came together unto Pilate, saying, Sir, we remember that that deceiver said, while He was yet alive, After three days I will rise again. Command therefore that the sepulchre be made sure until the third day, lest His disciples come by night, and steal Him away, and say unto the people, He is risen from the dead; so the last error shall be worse than the first. Pilate said unto them, Ye have a watch: go your way, make it as sure as ye can" (Matthew 27:62-65).

The swoon theory regarding the resurrection of our Lord asserts that Christ was removed from the cross by His friends before He had died, and that He was revived by the coolness of the tomb, from which He later arose. A definite refutation of this is found in the fact that His death and His burial were authoritatively acknowledged by both the Roman and Jewish governments.

That the resurrection was well known to the Jewish authorities is obvious. Nevertheless, these authorities made no attempt to refute the story of the resurrection. After the Lord arose, "there was a great earthquake: for the angel of the Lord descended from heaven, and came and rolled back the stone. . . . For fear of him the keepers did shake, and became as dead men. . . . Some of the watch came into the city, and showed unto the chief priests all the things that were done. And when they were assembled with the leaders, and had taken counsel, they gave large money unto the soldiers, Saying, Say ye, His disciples came by night, and stole Him away while we slept. And if this come to the governor's ears, we will persuade him, and secure you" (Matthew 28:1-24).

The resurrection of Christ is attributed to God the Father. "The mighty power [of God] wrought in Christ, when He raised Him from the dead" (Ephesians 1:19-20). The Lord

Jesus, the Eternal Son, stated that He Himself had power to rise again from the dead. He said, "I lay down My life, that I might take it again. No man taketh it from Me. . . . I have power to take it again. This commandment have I received of My Father" (John 10:17-18). The Spirit of God also shared a part in the triumph. "He [Christ was] put to death in the flesh, but quickened [made alive] by the Spirit (1 Peter 3:18).

An Attested Fact

Most of the witnesses prominent in the case were hesitant to believe in Christ's resurrection. We read concerning them: "Then all the disciples forsook Him and fled" (Matthew 26:56). How embarrassed they would be to see Him again! Peter naturally would be reluctant, for he had denied having known the Lord (Matthew 26:67-75). Incredulous Thomas would never have believed in the resurrection had it not been real and true and fully confirmed by personal observation (John 20:26-29). All of these would have disbelieved had there not been convincing evidence. Reality forced them to witness to the facts. Christ arose.

The Circumstances

There are several interesting circumstances which demand close attention:

1. *The circumstance of the empty tomb.* Evidently it previously had not been used, nor was it used afterwards. The fact that only one niche to contain a body is seen completed, and yet this niche is empty, should be accepted as a proof that our Lord arose.

Obviously the Lord was not in any hurry when He arose. When Peter and John entered the tomb, all had been left in perfect order. John came first to the sepulcher: "And he stooping down, and looking in, saw the linen clothes lying; yet went he not in. Then cometh Simon Peter following him, and went into the sepulchre, and seeth the linen clothes lie. And the napkin, that was about His head, not lying with the linen clothes, but wrapped together in a place by itself" (John 20:5-7).

Dr. W. H. Griffith Thomas in his volume, *Christianity Is Christ,* quotes Chrysostom:

> If the body had been stolen they could not have stolen it naked, because of the delay in stripping it of the burial cloths and the trouble caused by the drugs adhering to it.

He then himself adds:

> There is therefore no other possibility but that the body was taken out of the tomb by supernatural power.[1]

2. *The transformation in the disciples.* The men who previous to the death and resurrection of Christ were timid, fearful of being considered His associates, and incredulous, suddenly became fearless, and with boldness they bore witness to the resurrection. The only plausible explanation of this spiritual and psychological change in the personalities and characters of these men lies in the resurrection and power of the risen Christ. Even afterwards these disciples boldly preached Jesus and the resurrection.

Dr. Thomas writes:

> The next line of proof to be considered is the transformation of the disciples caused by the resurrection. They had seen their Master die, and through that death they lost all hope. Yet hope returned three days after. On the day of the crucifixion they were filled with sadness; on the first day of the week their hearts glowed with certainty and hope. When the message of the resurrection first came they were incredulous and hard to be convinced, but when they became assured they never again doubted. What could account for the astonishing change in these men in so short a time?[2]

---

[1]W. H. Griffith Thomas, *Christianity Is Christ,* page 74.

[2]Ibid, page 79.

3. *The silence of the authorities.* It is unbelievable that the Jewish authorities who had bribed the temple guards into silence should not vigorously protest the preaching of the apostles, had they thought the body of Jesus stolen. Why did they not make search, find, and produce it? Their silence and their inaction particularly form another circumstantial proof of the resurrection. Their only attempt was to silence the preaching and the contention of the apostles that Jesus was indeed risen, but this was very weak. They had no rebuttal to the claims that "Christ is risen from the dead" (1 Corinthians 15:20).

Professor Fairbairn says:

> The silence of the Jews is as significant as the speech of the Christians.[1]

4. *The physical appearances of our Lord after His resurrection.* It is true that on one of these occasions the disciples were "terrified and affrighted, and supposed that they had seen a spirit." But the Lord "said unto them, Why are ye troubled? and why do thoughts arise in your hearts? Behold My hands and My feet, that it is I Myself: handle Me, and see; for a spirit hath not flesh and bones, as ye see Me have" (Luke 24:34-39).

The Lord was no phantom. He appeared to His own in flesh and having the bone structure of an erect and perfect man. He talked to them, ate with them, and in fact cooked for them. He was no specter.

After rising from the dead He appeared physically to some of those who had known Him best. The first of these was Mary Magdalene. He said unto her, "Mary," and she replied, "Rabboni," for she certainly recognized Him. He then appeared to other women who immediately knew Him and worshiped Him.

---

[1]Patrick Fairbairn, *Studies in the Life of Christ,* page 357.

Both Luke and the Apostle Paul record an appearance of the risen Lord to Peter (Luke 24:34; 1 Corinthians 15:5). Perhaps this first contact had to be in private—there were delicate matters with which they had to deal.

Probably a little later the Lord appeared to two dejected friends on the way to Emmaus. He showed Himself to them at the evening meal, "and they knew Him." They then hurried to Jerusalem, and found the other disciples, saying, "The Lord is risen indeed" (Luke 24:35).

The Lord likewise appeared to all His disciples one day. Thomas, who was so skeptical about the resurrection, quickly recognized Him, and exclaimed, "My Lord and my God" (John 20:24-28).

To all these "He showed Himself alive after His passion by many infallible proofs, being seen of them forty days, and speaking of the things pertaining to the kingdom of God" (Acts 1:3).

5. One of the most convincing proofs of the resurrection is *the radical change in Mary's family.* The Lord had four brothers: James, Joses, Simon, and Judas, and He had at least two sisters (Matthew 13:55-56). Of these we read, "Neither did His brethren believe in Him" (John 7:5). In view of the whole story, it is difficult to accept that the condition of unbelief resulted from mere prejudice, rather than from confirmed incredulity.

Why was their mother left destitute and alone during the greatest crisis of her family life, the execution of her eldest child? Obviously there was more than prejudice in their minds. It seems definitely that they did not believe in His deity or in His Messiahship. They probably concurred secretly with the charge of blasphemy before the Jewish court and the charge of treason before the Roman governor, Pilate. Consequently they absented themselves at their brother's death.

Between the crucifixion and the beautiful family picture

portrayed as it was just before Pentecost, a stupendous event transpired. Paul records that after His resurrection Jesus was seen of Cephas (Peter), then of the twelve, of five hundred brethren at one time. "After that, He was seen of James" (1 Corinthians 15:5-8). From then on there was a manifest change, not only in James but in all "His brethren." James who did not believe in Him, now speaks of Christ as "the Lord Jesus Christ" (James 1:1), and as "our Lord Jesus Christ . . . of glory" (2:1).

What brought about this tremendous conversion? The resurrection.

In the prayer meeting preparatory to Pentecost "all continued with one accord in prayer and supplication, with the women, and Mary the mother of Jesus, and with His brethren" (Acts 1:14). At last they were a united family in the Lord.

6. *The existence of the Christian Church.* Before His death and resurrection the Lord Jesus declared concerning Peter's confession of Him, "Upon this rock I will build My church; and the gates of hell shall not prevail against it" (Matthew 16:18). Had Christ died and remained in the tomb, the apostolic nucleus of the Church would not have survived. Some of these did indeed return to their former vocation (John 21:3).

Since Pentecost the powers of hell have attempted to destroy the Church. Over and above periodic pressure opposing the development of the Church, three particular persecutions have been suffered by the Christians, all from different sources.

The first was from *a Jewish source* and was conducted under the leadership of a fanatic, Saul of Tarsus, a former student of Gamaliel. So zealous was this antagonist of Christianity that we read of his "breathing out . . . slaughter against the disciples of the Lord" (Acts 9:1).

Years later, as he reviewed this period of his life, Paul said to the Galatians, "Ye have heard of my conversation [way of living] in time past in the Jews' religion, how beyond measure I persecuted the church of God, and wasted it" (Galatians 1:13). Toward the end of his life, he deeply regretted his early activities: "I verily thought with myself, that I ought to do many things contrary to the name of Jesus. . . . Which thing I also did in Jerusalem: and many of the saints did I shut up in prison, having received authority from the chief priests; and when they were put to death, I gave my voice [vote] against them" (Acts 26:9-10).

Such then was the first concerted effort of "the gates of hell" to prevail against the Christian Church (Matthew 16:18).

The second persecution, a protracted one, came from *a heathen source—pagan Rome.* This persecution was waged against the people of God and stretched from the day of Nero (A.D. 64) through ten Roman emperors. These wicked men were: Nero, Domitian, Trajan, Antoninus, Severus, Maximinus, Decius, Valerian, Aurelian, and the very brutal Diocletian who decreed that not only were the Christians to be destroyed, but all their sacred writings as well.

This is what has been called the Smyrna period of church history. There is a probable reference to it in the Lord's epistle to the angel of the Church at Smyrna: "Ye shall have tribulation ten days: be thou faithful unto death, and I will give thee a crown of life" (Revelation 2:10).

It is estimated that hundreds of thousands of the Lord's faithful were martyred during this period; some by fire, some by sword, and some by wild beasts. Well does the Word of God describe the brutality of Roman society of those approximately three hundred years: "Full of envy, murder, debate, deceit, malignity; whisperers, backbiters, haters of God, despiteful, proud, boasters, inventors of evil things" (Romans 1:29-30).

During the Dark Ages another severe religious persecution

broke against the genuine Church of our Lord Jesus. Its source was really *papal Rome.* The Spanish Inquisition with its rack, its principal instrument of torture, and other means of physical and mental agony, will remain as a witness to Satan's attempts to "persecute and waste" the Church.

The records of factual history regarding the Hussites, the Waldenses, and the Huguenots, may be forgotten, but they cannot finally be obliterated. These disgraceful accounts have been indelibly written and will ever so remain. The existence of the Church today is a proof not only of the fact of the resurrection of Christ but of the power of that resurrection in and through the Lord Jesus.

7. *Further transformed lives.* The permanent transformation of the life of Saul of Tarsus is another proof of the resurrection of Christ. He states that on the day of his conversion he saw the Lord Jesus in glory. It was this sight of a risen and ascended Lord Jesus that changed the enemy of the Church into her greatest propagandist and supporter.

It was the sight of the same risen and exalted Lord that imparted strength to the protomartyr Stephen (Acts 7:56). Transformed lives become the material from which the Church is built (1 Peter 2:1-12). Throughout all the Christian centuries lives have been changed, and hearts have longed to know more of Christ and more of the power of His resurrection (Philippians 3:10).

What assurances these lives give that the Lord Jesus ever lives in the power of an endless life (Hebrews 7:16).

8. *The memorials.* Throughout the centuries of the Christian Church, two ordinances have been practiced, baptism and the Lord's Supper. Both of these are witnesses to the resurrection of the Lord Jesus. In baptism the believer is identified with Christ in His death, burial, and resurrection. The multitudes who have submitted to this ordinance have done so because they believed in the resurrection of Christ. They

were "buried with Him by baptism unto death; that like as Christ was raised up from the dead by the glory of the Father, even so we also should walk in newness of life" (Romans 6:4). Furthermore, baptism likewise foreshadows the resurrection of the believer. "For if we believe that Jesus died and rose again, even so them also which sleep in Jesus will God bring with Him [from among the dead]" (1 Thessalonians 4:14).

The Lord's Supper presupposes both the resurrection and the ascension of Christ for it is celebrated with a view to His return: "For as often as ye eat this bread, and drink this cup, ye do show the Lord's death till He come" (1 Corinthians 11:26).

These two ordinances are a perpetual testimony that there are thousands which have believed and do believe that Jesus Christ rose from the dead.

9. *The Lord's day.* The only explanation of the quick change in the minds and practice of the early Christians from the observation of the Jewish Sabbath to the first day of the week lies in the belief in the resurrection of Christ.

Previous to the crucifixion of the Lord the disciples kept the Sabbath. They even rested on the Sabbath day that Christ was in the tomb: "They returned, and prepared spices and ointments; and rested the Sabbath day according to the commandment" (Luke 23:56).

Almost immediately after His resurrection the same disciples met on the first day of the week: "Then the same day at evening [the evening of the resurrection], being the first day of the week, when the doors were shut where the disciples were assembled for fear of the Jews, came Jesus and stood in the midst, and saith unto them, Peace be unto you" (John 20:19). Within a short time they were meeting on that day to break bread: "Upon the first day of the week, when the disciples came together to break bread, Paul preached unto them" (Acts 20:7). Paul encouraged them to contribute their offerings, apparently on the same occasions: "Upon the first day of the week let every one of you lay by him in store, as God hath prospered him" (1 Corinthians 16:2).

The observation of the first day of the week by the Christian Church is a constant reminder, and is an evidence of the resurrection of Christ.

There was one point on the battlefield of Waterloo which was taken three times during that memorable day. Both Napoleon and Wellington realized the strategical importance of the position and concentrated attention upon it. Its ultimate possession and retention by the British troops contributed largely to the final results. In the same way, there is one point in connection with Christianity which from the first has been felt to be vital and central—the resurrection.[1]

Heresies Regarding the Resurrection

Rationalism refuses to accept a literal physical resurrection but, strange to say, it attempts to explain the appearances of Christ to His own after His resurrection. Rationalism is the philosophy that considers human reason alone sufficient to solve all the problems relating to man's nature and destiny. It makes the human mind supreme and rejects the supernatural and the miraculous. Inasmuch as the resurrection cannot be explained through man's reason, it is denied.

1. *The swoon theory.* This theory is an example of how far human reason will go in its denial of the miraculous. The theory holds that Christ did not actually die; that in the coolness of the tomb and by the fragrance of the spices He was revived. It is difficult to explain by this theory the long walk from Jerusalem to Emmaus and how, during that walk, He talked to friends by the way, and opened to them the Scriptures (Luke 24:32). It is incredible that one so brutally hurt, and one recovering from a deep swoon (supposedly),

---

[1]W. H. Griffith Thomas, *Christianity Is Christ,* page 70.

would have such strength and engage in such an intriguing conversation.

The physical strength and the mental vigor of our Lord in arising from the tomb refutes every attempt to thus rationalize the resurrection.

2. *The fraud theory.* How bigoted man can be! The fraud theory is almost as old as the resurrection itself. The "watch" at the tomb was paid "large money" and instructed by the Jewish Council, "Say ye, His disciples came by night, and stole Him away while we slept. And if this come to the governor's ears, we will persuade him, and secure you. So they took the money and did as they were taught" (Matthew 28:12-15).

That such a theory would be accepted by any today can only result from an ignorance of Biblical text.

3. *The vision theory.* This theory maintains that Mary Magdalene and the others suffered from hallucinations, and only thought that they had seen the Lord. Such folly is worthy of very little comment. While we readily concede that one might suffer from hallucinations, it is impossible to believe that over five hundred persons could all have hallucinations at the same time and in the same place. The Word of God states, "He [Christ] was seen of above five hundred brethren at once" (1 Corinthians 15:6). Furthermore, the Lord's last appearance to His disciples leaves no room for hallucinations. Here is reality: "Then the eleven disciples went away into Galilee, into a mountain where Jesus had appointed them. And when *they saw Him*, they worshipped Him: but some doubted. And Jesus came and spake unto them, saying, All power is given unto Me in heaven and in earth. Go ye therefore, and teach all nations" (Matthew 28:16-19).

4. *The gaseous theory.* This error has been adopted by at least one modern cult. Its contention is that the body of Jesus arose only in gases. What a contemptible prevarication!

Prophetically it was written of Christ, "Thou wilt not leave My soul in hell [here, sheol, the sphere of all the dead, impenitent and saved]; neither wilt Thou suffer Thine Holy One to see corruption" (Psalm 16:10). With Christ there would be no disintegration of the buried body.

Would Thomas, incredulous Thomas, have accepted such false teaching? When he saw the blessed Saviour's literal hands and side, he exclaimed, "My Lord, and my God!" It was no phantom that he saw; no spurious theory gripped his attention. Thomas knew that it was the Lord who stood before him, physically risen from among the dead.

Stepping out of the empty tomb, during a trip to the Holy Land, the author was thrilled to hear from the lips of a gathered crowd the words of that excellent, impressive hymn by Robert Lowry:

> Low in the grave He lay,
> Jesus, my Saviour,
> Waiting the coming day,
> Jesus, my Lord.
> Up from the grave He arose
> With a mighty triumph o'er His foes;
> He arose a Victor from the dark domain,
> And He lives forever with His saints to reign.

The resurrection is the cornerstone of any defense of the Christian faith. Upon it rests everything that is essential to Christian theology. Evidences for the resurrection are so abundant that they constitute one of the greatest apologetics for Christianity.[1]

Some Problems Regarding the Resurrection

The first step in the solution of any problem is to realize that one exists. In regard to the crucifixion and the resurrection of Christ problems must be admitted. On what day did He die? At what hour did He arise?

Without being dogmatic the following suggestions are

[1]John F. Walvoord, *Jesus Christ our Lord,* page 192.

given. They originally are not the author's.

The day of Christ's crucifixion. In searching for a solution to these questions various theories have been advanced. As to the crucifixion these theories respectively are called the Wednesday, the Thursday, and the Friday theories. In connection with the resurrection two theories have been suggested, the evening theory and the morning theory.

Tradition has designated Good Friday as the day on which the Lord Jesus died, the day before the Jewish Sabbath. It is generally accepted that the Jews asked that the body be removed from the cross before the Sabbath. We may well ask, which Sabbath?

Scripture and the calendar reveal that there were two Sabbaths in that week of our Lord's ministry, the passover week. The fifteenth day of that month, the day after the slaying of the paschal lamb, was a yearly Sabbath. We read, "In the fourteenth day of the first month at even is the LORD's passover. And on the fifteenth day of the same month is the feast of unleavened bread" (Leviticus 23:5-6). John says, "That sabbath day was an high day" (John 19:31). Matthew also makes reference to a plurality of Sabbaths, to which a further reference will be made.

The Jews were not allowed to prepare food on any sabbath day (Exodus 16:5,20-29). Therefore the day before "the high day" was called "the preparation of the passover" (John 19:14), and it was on that fateful day that Christ was crucified (John 19:13-18). Therefore, inasmuch as Saturday was the weekly Sabbath, and Friday was the passover Sabbath, Thursday must have been "the preparation of the passover," and that was the day Christ must have died.

These two Sabbaths coming together explains Matthew's statement, which is literally, "In the end of the sabbaths, as it began to dawn [draw] toward the first day of the week" (Matthew 28:1).[1]

[1]Roy M. Allen, *Three Days in the Grave,* New York: Loizeaux Brothers, 1942, page 22.

One other problem is worthy of note. The paschal lamb was not eaten until the passover Sabbath. The lamb was slain at even (Exodus 12:6; Deuteronomy 16:5-6) on Thursday, Nisan 14th, and the blood immediately sprinkled. The lamb was then roasted and eaten; and since the Jewish day ends and begins at 6 P.M. the passover feast was not until Nisan 15th, which must have been Friday.

From all this it must be concluded that, although the Lord had expressed the desire to eat the Passover with His disciples, He did not. The attitude of the Jewish authorities mentioned by John pinpoints the time of the passover feast for us: "Then led they Jesus from Caiaphas unto the hall of judgment: and it was early; and they themselves went not into the judgment hall, lest they should be defiled; but that they might eat the passover" (John 18:28).

A very important passage has been paraphrased:

> I have so greatly longed to be able to eat this passover with you before I suffer, but I must inform you that I may not, by any possibility, eat it while it should coincide with a prediction in the Kingdom of God.[1]

Obviously the supper that Christ ate with His disciples was the last meal of the day. A comparison of verses 1 and 29 of John 13 will show this.

In connection with the Lord's resurrection Matthew states that at the end of the Sabbath when the first day of the week began to dawn the women came to the sepulcher (Matthew 28:1). John tells that it was yet dark (John 20:1). Mark adds that it was at the early sunrise (Mark 16:2), and Luke says that it was very early (Luke 24:1).

As the women went in the semi-darkness of that very early morning, they met the guards on their way from the garden tomb to the city (Matthew 28:11). Before this meeting, prob-

---

[1]Ibid., pages 91-92.

ably just outside the Damascus gate, the guards had been shaken by the earthquake, they had seen the angels, and had fallen prostrate with fear. From these distressing experiences they had to recover, and this would naturally take time. They then had to walk to the city and the authorities. Taking all this into consideration, and knowing that the first day of the week, according to Jewish time, began at 6 P.M. Saturday evening, and that the Lord arose on the third day (1 Corinthians 15:4), we might assume that Christ arose, according to our time, on Saturday evening, the beginning of the Jewish first day of the week.

The Significance of the Resurrection

Any comprehensive understanding of the resurrection of Christ must entail a philosophy relative to the Lord Himself and to the results of His accomplishments culminating in His resurrection.

1. *The resurrection a proof of Christ's deity.* "Jesus Christ our Lord . . . of the seed of David [His humanity] . . . declared [marked out] to be the Son of God with power [His Deity], according to the Spirit of holiness, by the resurrection from the dead" (Romans 1:1-4). Inasmuch as the noun "dead" is in the plural, it may be that the resurrections performed during His public service are here viewed as culminating in His own. This then is the assurance of His sonship with God. He is the Victor over sin, death, and hell.

2. *The resurrection a vindication of Christ as Son of Man.* "This is an evil generation," said the Lord Jesus of the Jewish people. "They seek a sign; and there shall no sign be given it, but the sign of Jonas the prophet. For as Jonas was a sign unto the Ninevites, so shall the Son of man be to this generation" (Luke 11:29-30).

Jonah might easily have been considered by the Ninevites as a man back from the dead. What a sign! They apparently received his message as from a resurrected person. Christ in His death and resurrection is a similar sign to the Jewish nation. The Ninevites received Jonah; Israel has rejected the very Son of man to whom will be given "dominion, and glory, and a kingdom, that all people, nations, and languages, should serve Him" (Daniel 7:14). The risen Christ is indeed the Son of man.

3. *The resurrection is the demonstration of Christ's victory over death.* He said, "I am the first and the last, and the living one; and I became dead, and behold, I am living to the ages of the ages, and have the keys of death and of hades" (Revelation 1:17-18 JND). As the mighty Conqueror Christ has wrenched the keys, the power of death and hell, from Satan (compare with Hebrews 1:14). Those keys now dangle from the girdle of the victorious Seed of the woman whose heel was bruised, but who inflicted the head wound upon Satan that will eventually destroy him.

4. *The resurrection is the credential of the Lordship of Christ.* "To this end Christ both died, and rose, and revived, that He might be Lord both of the dead and the living" (Romans 14:9). Death ends all human lordships, but it is no barrier to the Lordship of Christ; He is Lord over all on both sides of the grave.

5. *The resurrection is the final qualification of the Judgeship of Christ.* "God," said the Apostle Paul to the men of Athens, ". . . commandeth all men every where to repent: Because He hath appointed a day, in the which He will judge the world in righteousness by that man whom He hath ordained: whereof He hath given assurance unto all men, in that He hath raised Him from the dead" (Acts 17:30-31).

God in grace and patience in past ages tolerated the ignorance of the Athenian pagans. Now through Paul He sent them a revelation of Himself and a call to repentance. He did this in order that they escape from the results of any rejection of His offer of grace. Eventually, through His risen and glorified Son He will judge the world in righteousness.

The resurrection of Christ in this passage appears first as the symbol of God's pledge to fulfill His prediction of judgment; and secondly as the qualification in Christ necessary for this office.

6. *The resurrection of Christ and His sovereignty.* While in the Holy Scriptures the sovereignty of Christ is based more upon His incarnation than upon His resurrection, it is obvious that had He not arisen from among the dead, He would have forfeited the right to worldwide dominion. It is of the risen glorified Lord Jesus that God declares: "Yet have I set My king upon My holy hill of Zion" (Psalm 2:6).

In the book of Revelation the testimony of Jesus is given (19:10-16). This is a witness concerning the blessed One whose human name is Jesus, the name upon the inscription over the cross. He is presented as a faithful and true Witness, and finally is called the King of kings and the Lord of lords.

7. *The resurrection of Christ and His high-priestly ministry.* This does not assume that Christ did not, previous to the resurrection, act as a priest. He is seen as such in the Epistle to the Hebrews (see Hebrews 1:3). Weymouth translates another passage from the same Epistle: "While every priest stands ministering day by day, and constantly offering the same sacrifices—though such can never rid us of sins—this Priest, on the contrary, after offering for sins a single sacrifice of perpetual efficacy, took His seat at God's right hand" (Hebrews 10:11-12).

In contrast to the constantly interrupted, by death, ministry of the Levitical priesthood, the ministry of the Lord Jesus is beyond death. His is a continual ministry; consequently, "He is able to save them to the uttermost that come unto God by Him" (Hebrews 7:25).

The Resurrection and the Believer

The resurrection of Christ is of major importance to the believer. It provides confirmation relative to spiritual experiences in the past and in the present, and to literal experiences predicted for the future.

1. *The resurrection and justification.* In writing to the saints at Rome, the Apostle Paul stated of the Lord Jesus, "Who was delivered for our offences, and was raised again for our justification" (Romans 4:25).

Justification is a change of man's state before God. This truth is closely related to the idea of a man being made righteous by God. The two words, "justification" and "righteousness," are derived from the same root and at times may be used interchangeably. Fenton in his work, *The New Testament in Current English* (not now so current as this work is dated in the 1880s), translates this verse, "Who was betrayed for our sins, and raised for our righteousness."[1] This, of course, would be the righteousness of Christ accredited to the believer on the principle of faith. Christ's resurrection assures us that the work that makes justification a blessed possibility has been completely finished.

2. *The resurrection and salvation.* "If thou shalt confess with thy mouth the Lord Jesus ["Jesus to be the Lord," says Dr. David Brown], and shalt believe in thine heart that God hath raised Him from the dead, thou shalt be saved" (Romans 10:9). Faith in the resurrection is faith in what man considers to be impossible; it is therefore strong unqualified confidence in God.

The resurrection is the basis of salvation. Here it also is a test of faith.

3. *The resurrection and the Christian life.* "We are [were, a past act] buried with [Christ] by baptism into death: that

---

[1]Ferrar Fenton, *The New Testament in Current English,* page 162.

like as Christ was raised up from the dead by the glory of the Father, even so we also should walk in newness of life'' (Romans 6:4). Since the believer has died to his old life, and since symbolically he has buried the old nature which sustained that life, now as risen with Christ, he is to walk in a new life of joy and holiness. The literal resurrection of Christ is the illustration of the spiritual resurrection of the Christian. The life of the risen Christ demonstrates what should characterize the new life of the believer.

4. *The resurrection and the gospel.* ''I delivered unto you first of all that which I also received, how that Christ died for our sins according to the scriptures; and that He was buried, and that He rose again the third day according to the scriptures'' (1 Corinthians 15:3-4). The gospel is news of a living Christ that gladdens the heart of the impotent and burdened sinner. ''If Christ be not raised, your faith is vain, ye are yet in your sins'' (1 Corinthians 15:17).

> Both history and our personal observation show that nothing can change the life and make men moral, like the gospel of free pardon in Jesus Christ. Mere preaching of morality will effect nothing of consequence. There never has been more insistence upon morality than in the most immoral times. . . . We do not become right by doing right, for only those can do right who have become right. . . . Justification is always accompanied by regeneration. Justification is followed by sanctification. All three are the result of the death and the resurrection of Christ.[1]

5. *The resurrection and the future.* ''If we believe that Jesus died and rose again, even so them also which sleep [in their graves] will God bring with Him [in resurrection]'' (1 Thessalonians 4:14). The time element between the resurrection of Christ and that of the believer is ignored. The resurrection of the Lord foreshadows the resurrection of all His own.

---

[1]A. H. Strong, *Systematic Theology*, page 863.

''Our conversation [mode of living] is in heaven; from whence also we look for the Saviour, the Lord Jesus Christ: Who shall change our vile body, that it may be fashioned like unto His glorious body, according to the working whereby He is able even to subdue all things unto Himself'' (Philippians 3:20-21).

8
MASTER, LORD, AND HEAD

"Rabbi," said Nicodemus, "We know that Thou art a teacher come from God," and in this we concur. That the Lord Jesus came from God, there is no doubt, nor is there any doubt that He was a great teacher.

The Teacher

The Lord Himself was fully conscious of His divine ability to teach and to instruct. In the upper room previous to His betrayal He said to His own, "Ye call Me Master [Teacher] and Lord: and ye say well; for so I am" (John 13:13). Our Lord was a very erudite and wise tutor. He sought to teach the people before His rejection and death. After His physical resurrection, He met with His own in Galilee and charged them saying, "Go ye therefore," or, "In going make disciples of all nations, baptizing them into the name of the Father, and of the Son, and of the Holy Spirit; teaching them to observe all things whatsoever I command you. And lo, I am with you all the days until the completion of the age. Amen" (Matthew 28:19-20 paraphrased).

"To teach," says the Oxford Dictionary, "is to explain, to show, and to state by way of instruction." A more expanded idea might be to communicate, to explain, to describe, to elucidate, and to illustrate. That the Divine Pedagogue used all such arts in His method of instruction is obvious.

How He Taught

There are few persons who can think abstractly, that is, to consider a matter apart from what is concretely known about that matter. The Lord Jesus knew this human trait, consequently *He taught pictorially.* Our Lord used figurative language very extensively. Readers of the Holy Scriptures find His imagery fascinating. He used similes, metaphors, allegories, and of course parables.

A simile is a brief comparison usually introduced by the comparative conjunction "as." A metaphor is a term used to describe an object to which it cannot literally apply. An allegory is an imaginary story used to illustrate another different subject; between them there is sufficient similitude for the first to throw light upon the second.

A parable is a story to illustrate by comparison. It always starts with a specific person and, although it may be fictitious, it is realistic in nature and details. Its purpose is to use the obvious to make clear the obscure. Some parables are single tales; others are more complex, a combination of short stories; as, for example, the stories of the lost sheep, the lost coin, and the lost son—all forming one parable (Luke 15:1-32). What delightful expedients our blessed Lord used in the arts of communication and instruction.

The records of the early ministry of our Lord direct us to *Judea* (John 2:13). While a period of public ministry there is implied in the statement of Nicodemus, "We know that Thou art a teacher come from God" (John 3:2), we understand through John the Apostle more of His private ministry in His conversation with Nicodemus and the woman at Sychar's well. It was in His conversation with the ruler of the Jews that He indicated the importance of the fundamental subject, the kingdom of God.

The ministry of our Lord was not confined to any enclosed

auditorium: "Jesus went about all Galilee, teaching in their synagogues, and preaching the gospel of the kingdom, and healing all manner of sickness and all manner of disease among the people" (Matthew 4:23).

The ministry of John the Baptist was given in the wilderness of Judea, not too far from the arid region of the Dead Sea. It was in these desert parts that the herald of the King lived and preached. In that parched and barren waste land the voice of the herald of the King, so stern and clear, announced the call of repentance to Judah.

In contrast, much of the ministry of the Lord Jesus was given around the beautiful Sea of Galilee, with its cool blue waters and its picturesque setting. "And He began to teach by the sea side: and there was gathered unto Him a great multitude, so that He entered into a ship, and sat in the sea; and the whole multitude was by the sea on the land" (Mark 4:1). Nestled in the bosom of that exquisitely lovely country there are sacred spots where the Master walked, stood, and taught the people, and where He healed their sick and comforted their sorrowing.

The final open area of Christ's ministry apparently was in *Perea* (John 10:40), during His last winter. John 9—12 covers much of His movements during those months. This thinly populated region provided Him with a place of retreat: "Jesus therefore walked no more openly among the Jews; but went thence unto a country near to the wilderness, into a city called Ephraim, and there continued with His disciples" (John 11:54). It was from there that He responded to the urgent call from Martha and Mary, after the death of Lazarus.

In all these parts *the Lord taught with authority*. He knew whereof He spoke, and transmitted His words with power.

When the Lord left the Temple the disciples asked for a private and detailed explanation of the prophecies that He had spoken. He therefore, in seclusion, elucidated certain features of eschatology. He gave them an understanding of the great tribulation period. To sum up His instructions, He used the fig tree as a visual aid. He then said, "Verily I say unto you, This generation shall not pass, till all these things be fulfilled. Heaven and earth shall pass away, but My words shall not pass away" (Matthew 24:34-35). The subjects which *the Lord taught were permanently fixed* in the purposes of God.

What He Taught

To list the many subjects which the Lord taught in the short time of His public service would require greater space than is available to us. Much of His material could be classified. For example, *He taught doctrine*: the doctrine of God, the doctrine of man, the doctrine of sin, and the doctrine of salvation. He in like manner tutored His own in *prophecy,* delineating for them the different stages of Daniel's seventieth week. Futhermore, He gave instructions in church matters.

The entire mission of our Lord, as well as His preaching, rested firmly upon the fact that "God is a Spirit infinite, eternal, and unchangeable" as the Westminster Confession reads. Since creation, God has revealed Himself to man: "That which may be known of God is manifest in them; for God hath showed it unto them. For the invisible things of Him from the creation of the world are clearly seen, being understood by the things that are made, even His eternal power and Godhead; so that they are without excuse" (Romans 1:19-20).

Regrettably, man rejected that revelation: "Because that, when they knew God, they glorified Him not as God, neither were thankful; but became vain in their imaginations, and their foolish heart was darkened. Professing themselves to be wise, they became fools'' (Romans 1:21-22).

Man since the fall in Eden has become an idolater and a pervert: ''Who changed the truth of God into a lie, and worshipped and served the creature more than the Creator, who is blessed forever. Amen. For this cause God gave them up into vile affections'' (Romans 1:25-26a). ''God gave them over to a reprobate mind, to do those things which are not convenient'' (Romans 1:28).

Man's eternal destiny depends upon either his obedience or disobedience to God. ''As by one man sin entered into the world, and death by sin; and so death passed upon all men, for that all have sinned [sinned in their federal head, Adam]'' (Romans 5:12). ''As by one man's disobedience many were made sinners, so by the obedience of one shall many be made righteous'' (Romans 5:19).

The consequence of man's sin is death in its spiritual, physical, and eternal aspects. The impenitent must experience what Scripture calls ''the second death.'' Those who by faith are in Christ shall be forever with the Lord.

Professor P. B. Fitzwater in his *Theology* quotes Dr. James Orr:

> Drug conscience as deeply as one may, a time comes when it awakes. Turn in what direction one will, sin confronts one as a fact in human life—an experience of the heart, a development in history, a crimson thread in literature, a problem for science, and an enigma for philosophy.[1]

Perhaps the subject the Lord dealt with most comprehensively was that of *the kingdom of God.* Of course He Himself is the King. The Old Testament practically closes with the announcement, ''Behold, I will send My messenger, and he shall prepare the way before Me'' (Malachi 3:1). Immediately after the genealogy of our Lord, the New Testament opens:

---

[1]P. B. Fitzwater, *Christian Theology,* page 320.

"In those days came John the Baptist, preaching in the wilderness of Judea, And saying, Repent ye: for the kingdom of heaven is at hand. For this is he that was spoken of by the prophet Esaias, saying, The voice of one crying in the wilderness, Prepare ye the way of the Lord, make His paths straight" (Matthew 3:1-3). Christ incarnate was and is the King, and John the baptist was His herald.

In the rejection of Christ as Messiah, the nation of Judah accepted a Roman emperor as their king. They cried, "We have no king but Caesar." For long centuries now that nation has suffered under the oppression and domination of the Gentiles, and will continue thus to suffer until the Lord Jesus Christ is accepted as Messiah, and a repentant and humbled people cry, "Hosanna: Blessed is the King of Israel that cometh in the name of the Lord" (John 12:13). "He shall be great, and shall be called the Son of the Highest: and the Lord God shall give unto Him the throne of His father David" (Luke 1:32).

According to Matthew (chapter 13) our Lord spoke seven parables which are related to the kingdom in its present form. These parables are called "the mysteries of the kingdom of Heaven." A Biblical mystery is a divine secret hidden by God in the past, but revealed mostly in apostolic times.

Professor Fitzwater writes concerning these mysteries of the kingdom:

> These parables clearly reveal the conditions in the world between Christ's crucifixion and His coming to establish His Kingdom. The first four were spoken to the mixed multitude, the last three to the disciples apart. He did not teach in parables till they had set their hearts against Him. After they had turned against Him and attributed His works to the devil, He denounced them in the most scathing terms and began to teach in parables. It is gross error to make the teaching of these parables church truth.[1]

---

[1]Ibid., page 539.

Salvation in its culminative aspect will be fully and joyfully experienced at the return of Christ: "Unto them that look for Him shall He appear the second time without sin unto salvation" (Hebrews 9:28).

Through a crucified and triumphant Saviour, "who was delivered for our offences and . . . raised again for our justification" (Romans 4:25), deliverance from divine wrath is procured for the believing sinner (Romans 5:9). Furthermore, there is forgiveness from sins for all such (Ephesians 1:7), and redemption from the curse of a broken law (Galatians 3:13-14). Through the accomplishments of Christ in His atonement, liberty from the power of sin is possible (Romans 8:2), and acceptance with God is assured (Ephesians 1:6).

Another great subject introduced by our Lord in the teaching of His own was that of *the Church.* As implied in the quotation from Professor Fitzwater, this doctrine must not be confused with kingdom truth.

The Lord when He was here on earth definitely stated that the building of His Church was yet future (Matthew 16:17-19). In His upper room ministry, He indicated that His Church was unique in her origin, character, and destiny. It is error to suggest that Adam, Enoch, and other Old Testament saints were in the Church. The Lord also intimated that it would be universal and that it would have a local aspect, properly administered (Matthew 18:15-18).

Much of His teaching in this regard was fulfilled on the Day of Pentecost (Acts 2), and still more was executed by the apostles (Ephesians 2:19-22).

The Lord

The title lord, as used among men, was bestowed in ancient times by the king upon the heads of clans and prominent families. It carried with it a certain authority from the reigning monarch. In England this title has survived as a token of high favor, although much of its former power and privilege have disappeared. It is used today as an expression of courtesy and high esteem for those honored by, and serving in some capacity, the sovereign of the realm.

The Title Lord in Scripture

When the title Lord is applied in Scripture to the Son of God it implies full power and absolute authority. The title Master, also given to Christ, when it is a translation of the Greek word *despotēs* indicates one who possesses supreme authority.

There are several Hebrew and Greek words in the Bible, all of which are translated into English by the title Lord. Two of these are very important and must be considered. One is found in the Old Testament, the other in the New.

The title Lord in the Old Testament. When the title Lord in the KJV of the Old Testament is spelled out in small capital letters it is the translation of the name Jehovah. This is the important name that we must consider.

Among the Hebrew people this name demands and receives the highest reverence and awe. In the public reading of the Scriptures the name Jehovah is not articulated. Either another name for God is substituted or the reader simply pauses. In this manner the name Jehovah is deeply revered.

The name LORD, Jehovah, in the Old Testament means the constantly-existing self-existing One. The word Jehovah is derived from the Hebrew verb to be, to exist.

The Lord revealed Himself to Moses at the burning bush as "I am that I am" (Exodus 3:14). When this concept of the Lord is transferred to the New Testament it is expressed by the clause, "Him which is, and which was, and which is to come" (Revelation 1:4,8).

In referring to the incarnation of Christ frequently speakers and teachers quote the words of the Apostle Paul, "Great is the mystery of godliness: God was manifest in the flesh" (1 Timothy 3:16). There is sufficient evidence in the Bible to paraphrase this, "Great is the mystery of Lordship, Jehovah was manifest in the flesh." The Word of God leaves no doubt that Jesus of Nazareth was Jehovah incarnate. A comparison of certain passages of the Old Testament with some in the New will prove this. Shortly before His birth Jesus is referred to as Jehovah. Isaiah predicting the ministry of John the Baptist avers, "Prepare ye the way of the LORD [Jehovah], make straight in the desert a highway for our God" (Isaiah 40:3). The sentiment of these words are applied by Luke to the Lord Jesus (Luke 1:76). A comparison of Isaiah 6:1-5; 53:1 with John 12:37-41 fully proves that Jesus was indeed Jehovah in His character and ministry. He is referred to as Jehovah in His death and resurrection. This is readily seen by a comparison of Judges 5:12-13 and Psalm 68:17-18 with Ephesians 4:7-10. There are a number of Scriptures which may be compared in order to demonstrate the contention that Jesus is in very truth Jehovah LORD.

Inasmuch as the fact is established that Jehovah in the Old Testament is indeed Jesus in the New, let us consider the title Lord in the New Testament.

The title Lord in the New Testament. There is more than one Greek title translated into English by the word Lord, but again, as in the Old Testament there is one more prominent than the others, so is it in the New, and this is the Greek title *kurios.* There are a few salient points regarding this title which demand attention.

The translators of the Septuagint Version of the Old Testament always used this Greek word *kurios* as the equivalent of Jehovah.

The title *kurios* conveys some very specific ideas: first, it implies ownership (Luke 19:33; Matthew 20:8; Galatians

4:1). Secondly, it indicates jurisdiction (Matthew 6:24; 24:50; Ephesians 6:5). Thirdly, it imposes absolute rule and authority (the rule and authority of a Caesar). An example of this meaning is seen in the words of Festus to King Agrippa about Paul and his appeal for justice to Caesar: "Of whom I have no certain thing to write unto my lord" (Acts 25:26). It is also seen in the title of our Lord Jesus: "The Lamb shall overcome them: for He is Lord of lords, and King of kings: and they that are with Him are called, and chosen and faithful" (Revelation 17:14).

The full import of this august title must be understood as involving the fact that Christ is the divine possessor, that He has complete jurisdiction over all that He possesses, and that He governs and controls all that He possesses with supreme and absolute power.

Our Lord Jesus Christ

There is a point which many of God's people have not noticed, and that point is of significance. There are only a few references in the Scriptures to the Lord by His personal name, Jesus. His immediate disciples did not address Him by that personal name. Such exclamations as: "It shall not be unto Thee, Lord!" "Lord, why cannot I follow Thee now?" "It is the Lord!" "My Lord and my God!" are classic examples of the use of this title. Let us keep them in mind.

John and Luke use the Lord's personal name in recording historical events. The pagans made reference to the Lord as Jesus. They said, "These all do contrary to the decrees of Caesar, saying that there is another king, one Jesus" (Acts 17:7). The Lord used it once concerning Himself, and in so doing He came very near to His own as He closed the canon of full revelation: "I Jesus have sent Mine angel to testify unto you these things in the churches" (Revelation 22:16).

Let all therefore follow the example of the disciples, the apostles of Christ, and address Him ever as Lord.

There are several adaptations of this title when it is applied to Christ which merit examination.

"The Lord from Heaven" (1 Corinthians 15:47). In this passage the Lord Jesus stands in contrast to Adam: "The first man is of the earth, earthy: the second man is the Lord from heaven." What an unfolding of the Divine Essence! As the Lord from Heaven He must have been preexistent; His origin must have been heavenly and therefore stands in contrast to man's origin. How great was His condescension!

The Lord Jesus on one occasion said to the Pharisees, "Ye are from beneath, I am from above: ye are of this world; I am not of this world" (John 8:23).

May we have the submissive will of John the Baptist, who said, "He must increase, but I must decrease. He that cometh from above is above all" (John 3:30-31).

The Lord of Glory. Another lesson through contrast may be learned from the two references to Christ as "the Lord of glory." In the first we are reminded of the appalling ignorance of men in the world about the person and character of the Lord Jesus: "The hidden wisdom . . . which none of the princes of this world knew: for had they known it, they would not have crucified the Lord of glory" (1 Corinthians 2:7-8). This passage records the nefarious attitude and act toward the Lord Jesus when that glory was veiled.

In the second reference, James 2:1, the half brother of our Lord expresses his love and esteem, his appreciation and understanding of the One who was raised in the family with him.

Throughout his early manhood James and his brothers were unbelievers. We read, "Neither did His brethren believe in Him" (John 7:5). Apparently James did not become a believer until after the resurrection (1 Corinthians 15:7).

After his conversion James became a bond slave of God and of the Lord Jesus Christ. He so speaks in his Epistle: "James, a servant [bond slave] of God and of the Lord Jesus Christ" (James 1:1). Throughout the remainder of his life, he revered and exalted the Son of God. He cautioned Hellenistic converts, "My brethren, have not the faith of our Lord Jesus Christ . . . of glory, with respect of persons" (James 2:1).

The title "Lord Jesus Christ of Glory" suggests that the Lord Jesus is the personification of the Shekinah, the visible glory of Jehovah that rested upon the mercy seat and was seen as a pillar cloud by day and a fiery cloud by night. We must also exalt Him who is the radiation of the Eternal Glory.

The Lord of Hosts. The title Lord of Sabaoth in the New Testament is exactly the same as the LORD (Jehovah) of Hosts in the Old Testament. This is the only Jehovic title to pass from the one Testament to the other. It is one of the compound titles of Jehovah that does not appear until the days of David. Frequently it is found in David's experiences and writings. David said to Goliath, "Thou comest to me with a sword, and with a spear, and with a shield: but I come to thee in the name of the LORD of hosts, the God of the armies of Israel, whom thou hast defied" (1 Samuel 17:45).

Jacob's eyes were opened to see his divine defenders from Esau and his four hundred armed men: "And Jacob went on his way, and the angels of God met him. And when Jacob saw them, he said, This is God's host" (Genesis 32:1-2).

In his vision Isaiah saw Jehovah "upon a throne, high and lifted up." He also heard one seraph saying to another, "Holy, holy, holy, is the LORD of hosts: the whole earth is full of His glory" (Isaiah 6:1-5).

These Old Testament references all indicate that the Lord is supreme over all celestial hosts. Furthermore, they also reveal that these invisible hosts are ready to fly at the command of their Lord to do His bidding. As in the case of Jacob and of David, they are prompt in the defense of those in danger. The Lord sends them forth "to minister for them who shall be heirs of salvation" (Hebrews 1:14).

The context in which the title "the Lord of Sabaoth [the Lord of Hosts]" is found in the Epistle of James should encourage many of God's people "in the last days" when there is such a struggle between capital and labor. "The cries of them that have reaped [without proper remuneration] have entered into the ears of the Lord of sabaoth," the protector of His people (James 5:5).

King of kings and Lord of lords. It seems appropriate that we consider this superb title of Christ in His kingdom glory. Nebuchadnezzar asserted that even now He is Lord of kings, and that as such He holds in secret His movements among the nations, and reveals only to a few what He is doing. Throughout all time, "The most High ruleth in the kingdom of men, and giveth it to whomsoever He will, and setteth up over it the basest of men" (Daniel 4:17).

When Christ returns in power and great glory He will subjugate all human rulers. No matter how many kings there may be among the nations, the Lord will be King over them all. No matter how many lords there may be used in the administration of national affairs under these kings, Christ will be Lord over them all.

This title indicates the supreme sovereignty of the Lord Jesus when all things will be put under Him. The day is coming when every pernicious policy, every oppressive act, every evil intention, and every enslaving system will be crushed as with a rod of iron. The Lord Jesus in triumph will be set upon the holy hill of Zion. Then shall the earth rejoice. In anticipation of that future event John writes, "I heard as it were the voice of a great multitude, and as the voice of many waters, and as the voice of mighty thunderings, saying, Alleluia: for the Lord God omnipotent reigneth" (Revelation 19:6).

"And He hath on His vesture and on His thigh a name written, KING OF KINGS AND LORD OF LORDS" (Revelation 19:16).

The Claims of Christ

During the few years of His public ministry, the Lord Jesus made claims of tremendous importance: first, He claimed to be the Son of God: "I and My Father are one. Then the Jews took up stones again to stone Him. Jesus answered them, many good works have I showed you from My Father; for which of those works do ye stone Me? The Jews answered Him, saying, For a good work we stone Thee not; but for blasphemy; and because that Thou, being a man, makest Thyself God" (John 10:30-32).

In the second place He claimed to be the Judge of all mankind: "For as the Father hath life in Himself; so hath He given to the Son to have life in Himself and hath given Him authority to execute judgment also, because He is the Son of man" (John 5:26-27).

Christ also accepted the role of King, the Messiah of Israel. When Pilate asked the Lord Jesus, "Art Thou the King of the Jews? Jesus said unto him, Thou sayest" (Matthew 27:11). The Apostle John in his Gospel amplifies this by adding these words to the statement of Christ, "To this end was I born" (John 18:37).

The Lord Jesus in like manner announced Himself as the Saviour of the world, the Redeemer of men: "The Son of man came not to be ministered unto, but to minister, and to give His life a ransom for many" (Matthew 20:28). "For the Son of man is come to seek and to save that which was lost" (Luke 19:10). Let one more of these important claims of Christ be sufficient: He certainly claimed to be the Lord and Master of His disciples. In the upper room He said, "Ye call Me Master and Lord: and ye say well; for so I am" (John

13:13). The disciples called Him Lord (*Kurios*) and Teacher (*Didaskalos*). Christ was their Governor and Instructor. What a happy relationship.

The Lordship of Christ

Before an examination of the Lordship of Christ over the Christian Church is undertaken, attention should be given to at least three weighty points:

The Lordship of Christ and His resurrection. The full significance of the Lordship of Christ in the gospel and over the entire Church rests upon His triumphant resurrection. Peter on the Day of Pentecost said, "God hath made that same Jesus whom ye crucified, both Lord and Christ" (Acts 2:36). The Apostle Paul wrote to the saints at Rome, "To this end Christ . . . died, and rose, and revived, that He might be Lord both of the dead and living" (Romans 14:9).

We are not to judge another brother, Paul states, because "to his own master he standeth or falleth" (Romans 14:4). The believer has been purchased, his redemption price has been paid, consequently his Lord and Master is the One who died for him and rose again. As the possessor of all the redeemed, Christ the Lord is the Judge of motives, attitudes, and actions: "To this end Christ both died, and rose."

The Lordship of Christ is unlimited. From Paul's words to the saints at Rome it is obvious that there are no limitations to the Lordship of Christ. Those who have been made lords by earthly sovereigns cease so to be at death. Furthermore, their power is imposed by them only upon the living. No restrictions limit the powers of Christ's Lordship. He has triumphed over death and lives in the power of an endless life. He therefore imposes His Lordship upon all on both sides of the grave, the dead and the living.

The Lordship of Christ is imposed upon all. In writing to

the Corinthians the Apostle Paul declared, "To them that are sanctified in Christ Jesus, called to be saints, with all that in every place call upon the name of Jesus Christ our Lord, both theirs and ours" (1 Corinthians 1:2). None of God's people have an exclusive right to the Lord: He belongs to all His own, and He exercises His Lordship upon everyone who has called upon His name.

The Lordship of Christ and spiritual enablement. The apostle in writing further to the Corinthians draws a vivid contrast between what they had been before conversion and what they had become since. They had been led by different spurious arts and means, but always toward idolatry. Pagan philosophies led them deeper into pagan worship. Through Christianity they had one divine Leader, the Holy Spirit, and He always led them in one direction: to acknowledge Christ as Lord. The New Translation significantly reads, "No one speaking in [the power of the] Spirit of God, says, Curse [on] Jesus; and no one can say, Lord Jesus, unless in [the power of the] Holy Spirit" (1 Corinthians 12:3 N.T.). The Spirit of God is the divine enablement in the Christian to own Christ as Lord over life in all its changes.

The Lord of Christians

"Sanctify the Lord in your hearts" (1 Peter 3:15) is an imperative by the Apostle Peter. It was written primarily to those who were called upon to suffer for the testimony of Christ. The New Translation reads, "Sanctify [the] Lord the Christ in your hearts." Many believe that Peter here was quoting the words of Isaiah: "Sanctify the Lord [Jehovah] of hosts Himself; and let Him be your fear, and let Him be your dread" (Isaiah 8:13). If this assumption is correct, then Peter here acknowledges that "the Lord, the Christ" is One no less than Jehovah of Hosts.

The idea of sanctifying the Lord in our hearts seems to be

an Old Testament concept. Speaking of Israel, God said, "I will be sanctified in them. . . . I will be hallowed [sanctified] among the children of Israel" (Leviticus 10:3; 22:32).

Leviticus is the book of the sanctuary and of the priesthood. In this remarkable book God is teaching Israel that those who approach into His presence must be aware of His infinite holiness, and therefore must reverence and fear the Lord.

Dr. Mason in Ellicott's *Commentary* has a very helpful note:

> To glorify God means to recognize His glorious perfections. To magnify Him means to recognize His greatness. To justify Him is to recognize His inherent justice. To sanctify His name means to recognize in word and deed His infinite holiness.[1]

To recognize God's infinite holiness is to conduct oneself in holiness and purity before God. To sanctify the Lord Jesus in our hearts is to make our hearts sanctuaries for Him. Within our hearts the Lord Jesus in His infinite holiness should be enshrined, and if He is there enshrined the results will be obvious.

Holiness of behavior. "As He which hath called you is holy, so be ye holy in all manner of conversation; because it is written, Be ye holy; for I am holy" (1 Peter 1:15).

Holiness has been defined as that quality of character that results from abstinence from evil. It is not merely a separation from sin, but the positive good that results from such a separation.

Peter's exhortation is in conflict with the ideals and practices of some who sincerely seek holiness. These imagine that holiness is to be found in a cloister or a convent, a place of isolation from the world. This imperative indicates differently; it exhorts the Christian to be holy in all manner of conver-

---

[1]*Ellicott's Bible Commentary: New Testament,* page 418.

sation, in every mode of living. The Christian is to be holy in every aspect of life.

Obedience to the Word of God. Paul uses a forceful paradox when writing about domestic difficulties: "I command, yet not I, but the Lord" (1 Corinthians 7:10). The command of the Lord was to be the end of all strife. Some might find fault with Paul's directive, but no one dare ignore the commandment of the Lord. His Word must be obeyed, otherwise serious consequences might follow. Samuel said to Saul, "Behold, to obey is better than sacrifice, and to hearken than the fat of rams" (1 Samuel 15:22). Paul very highly commends the saints at Philippi: "Wherefore, my beloved, as ye have always obeyed, not as in my presence only, but now much more in my absence" (Philippians 2:12). Few there are who have such a record of obedience in the things of God.

Job concludes that there is a true blessing in the obedience of God's instructions: "Behold, God is mighty, and despiseth not any. . . . If they obey and serve Him, they shall spend their days in prosperity, and their years in pleasures" (Job 36:5-11). Only when we enshrine the Lord in the sanctuary of our hearts by implicit obedience can we expect such a rich blessing.

A reverential fear of the Lord. One of the first proverbs in the divine collection reads, "The fear of the LORD is the beginning of knowledge" (Proverbs 1:7). Another is quite similar: "The fear of the LORD is the beginning of wisdom" (Proverbs 9:10).

The Christian has no slavish fear of the Lord, but knowing God in His infinity and in His moral attributes, he lives in awe and reverence before God.

The Head

There is another subject that is intimately related to the

Lordship of Christ; that is the Headship of Christ.

He is Head of all Creation. The Apostle Paul wrote to the Colossians, "Ye are complete [ye lack nothing as to your standing before God] in Him, which is the head of all principality and power" (Colossians 2:10). Christ alone possesses all universal power and authority (John 13:3; Matthew 28:18).

The erroneous teaching propagated in Colosse was the elevating of celestial beings to a place of veneration and worship. This spurious philosophy dishonored Christ, the Head of all creation and the Head of the Church.

Christ is the Head of every man. "I would have you know, that the head of every man is Christ; the head of the woman is the man; and the head of Christ is God" (1 Corinthians 11:3). There is a gradation in this divine scheme of headship from the lowest to the highest, from man through Christ to God.

In the plan of redemption each Person in the Godhead, although absolutely one in essence, in nature assumed temporarily a certain position in order that the plan of salvation be accomplished. The Father is sovereign, from whom all things proceed; the Son is the means by which all is procured; and the Holy Spirit is the agent by which all that is for the believer may be possessed.

God is the Head of Christ, Christ is the Head of man, and the man is the head of the woman. This is a system of headship which indicates an orderly arrangement of subjection.

Christ is the Head of the Church. The analogy of the human body is used by the Holy Spirit to teach the organic oneness of the Body of Christ, and the power that controls it.

The Apostle Paul stresses that the Church is the complementary part of Christ: "The church, which is His body, the fullness of Him that filleth all in all" (Ephesians 1:22-23). He also uses it to reveal the power that controls it:

"For as the body is one, and hath many members, and all the members of that one body, being many, are one body: so also is [the] Christ" (1 Corinthians 12:12). The Head is in Heaven, some of the members are also in Heaven, but some are still on earth; these together form the mystical Body of Christ.

The difference between lordship and headship may be stated quite simply. Lordship controls by decrees, but headship regulates by coordination. The lack of coordination between the human mind and body is a symptom of trouble, of disease. The attitude of some in the Church of the Colossians in not adhering to the Head, the Lord Jesus, indicated a departure from the truth of God, heresy.

9

THE PRESENT MINISTRY OF CHRIST

How dependent the Church of God is upon the present activities of the Lord Jesus. A better understanding of these may be derived from a close examination of certain titles which are applied to Him and certain aspects of His ministry. "For Christ is not entered into the holy places made with hands, which are the figures of the true; but into heaven itself, now to appear in the presence of God for us" (Hebrews 9:24). But first of all:

The Ascension

The historian Luke records two accounts of the ascension of the Lord Jesus, one in his Gospel, the other in his Church history, the book of the Acts. John Mark also gives a report. These three accounts vary somewhat. The Holy Spirit who indited them has selected precise language to describe our Lord's return to the Father. The descriptive words employed leave two impressions: one, that Christ ascended by an act of His own will and power; the other, that He was removed from earth by an appointment of the Father.

Luke's account in his Gospel furnishes some very interesting details; one, "While He blessed them, He was parted from them." One can only wonder if His blessing on that occasion was that of the Aaronic benediction which His disciples knew so well:

> The LORD bless thee, and keep thee:

The LORD make his face shine upon thee,
and be gracious unto thee:
The LORD lift up His countenance upon thee,
and give thee peace (Numbers 6:24-26).

If it were that benediction how much more meaningful these words would become to those apostles.

While discoursing with His disciples in the upper room, the Lord made a number of references to His ascension. He reminded them, "I go to the Father." He also revealed to them that certain benefits would accrue to them through His return to the Father. "Verily, verily, I say unto you, He that believeth on Me, the works that I do shall he do also; and greater works than these shall he do; because I go unto My Father" (John 14:12). These are astonishing words which must be understandable or otherwise they would not have been spoken. Were they to receive divine power as the result of the Lord's ascension? The message of the apostles was accompanied by supernatural power: "And by the hands of the apostles were many signs and wonders wrought among the people" (Acts 5:12).

Peter and John healed the poor mendicant at the gate of the Temple (Acts 3:1-9). Peter raised Dorcas to life again (Acts 9:36-43). The Apostle Paul performed a miracle of judgment on Elymas the sorcerer (Acts 13:6-12). These were similar to some of the works of the Lord Jesus, but what could He have meant by "Greater works than these shall he do"?

It has been suggested that this statement does not mean that the apostles would do works greater in their supernatural demonstration, but greater only in the extent. The works of our Lord were confined to one small nation; He never went beyond the frontiers of Palestine. How more extensive the missionary work of the apostles! Peter in Babylon, Paul and colleagues in Pisidia, Asia Minor, Macedonia, Galatia, etc.

If Church history and tradition are in anywise reliable, the other apostles spread throughout the then known world. Greater in extent were their accomplishments.

Another important advantage for the Church and, through the Church, for the world is the descent of the Holy Spirit. "I will pray the Father, and He shall give you another Comforter, that He may abide with you for ever; even the Spirit of truth" (John 14:16-17). In a further discourse the Lord said, "It is expedient for you that I go away: for if I go not away, the Comforter will not come unto you. . . . And when He is come, He will reprove the world of sin, and of righteousness, and of judgment: Of sin, because they believe not on Me [the culmination of all sin], Of righteousness, because I go to My Father [all the claims of Christ as to His deity and Messiahship are fully vindicated by the Father in that He raised Him from among the dead and seated Him at His own right hand in Heaven] . . . Of judgment, because the prince of this world is judged [this evil one is now awaiting final execution]" (John 16:7-11).

On the eve of His leaving His own, Christ said, "Peace I leave with you, My peace I give unto You: not as the world giveth, give I unto you. Let not your heart be troubled, neither let it be afraid. . . . I go unto the Father" (John 14:27-28).

On the great day of the atonement in Israel (Leviticus 16), the high priest, who had appeared on the north side of the altar to slay the goat taken for the Lord, entered into the sanctuary and there appeared in the presence of God for His people; so is it with the Lord Jesus.

For His Church the Lord Jesus is the Last Adam, the Capstone of the corner, the Head of the Church, the Great and Chief Shepherd, the Great High Priest and Advocate, the Forerunner, and the Bridegroom.

The Last Adam

This significant title is found in the context of the resurrection: "The first man Adam was made a living soul; the Last Adam . . . a quickening Spirit" (1 Corinthians 15:45). What a vivid contrast!

Of the first man Adam the Word of God relates, "The LORD God formed man of the dust of the ground, and breathed into his nostrils the breath of life; and man became a living soul" (Genesis 2:7). Alas, through man's fall "sin entered into the world, and death by sin" (Romans 5:12). Consequently, "in Adam all die" (1 Corinthians 15:22). Furthermore, all Adam's progeny are "sons of disobedience" (Ephesians 2:2). His act of disobedience is here viewed as the paternal origin of his sinful progeny.

Adam's sin not only thus affected himself and all his descendants but creation as well. "Unto Adam [the Lord] said . . . Cursed is the ground for thy sake; in sorrow shalt thou eat of it all the days of thy life; thorns also and thistles shall it bring forth to thee; and thou shalt eat the herb of the field" (Genesis 3:17-18).

These are some of the characteristics of the first literal creation of which Adam was the federal head.

There is a new creation of which our Lord Jesus Christ, the Last Adam, the Second Man, from Heaven is head, where "all things are of God, who hath reconciled us to Himself by Jesus Christ" (2 Corinthians 5:17-18). This is a spiritual creation. "If any man is in Christ he also is in that new creation." ("New" in the Greek here implies a new nature quite different from anything previously existing.[1]) The believer is created anew in Christ Jesus. Human effort or state is of no value in this new creation. "For in Christ Jesus neither circumcision availeth any thing, nor uncircumcision, but a new creature [creation]" (Galatians 6:15).

---

[1]Jamieson, Fausset, and Brown, *Commentary,* page 309.

For all who enter that new creation, "Old things are passed away; behold all things are become new. Some of the characteristics of the new creation over which the Last Adam is Lord are life, life more abundant (John 10:10), peace (John 14:27), joy (John 15:11). The Last Adam is indeed a life-giving spirit.

The Capstone of the Corner

The Apostle Peter probably retained clear recollections of his visit with the Master to Caesarea Philippi. It is unthinkable that he would forget that defiant declaration, "Thou art Peter, and upon this rock I will build My church; and the gates of hell shall not prevail against it" (Matthew 16:18). The Lord promptly declared how that Church would be built. He spoke of the material used in the superstructure and the purpose of that great spiritual edifice. It is in this connection that the apostle enables one to visualize the Lord Himself as the chief Cornerstone and the Headstone (Capstone) of the corner.

The Lord Jesus is not only the "rock" to which He made reference when He spoke to Peter; He is the only true foundation. "For other foundation can no man lay than that is laid, which is Jesus Christ" (1 Corinthians 3:11). He is the chief Cornerstone where two rectangular walls meet. There may be another important stone at the point where the opposite two rectangular walls join, but Christ is the chief Cornerstone.

As the Capstone of the corner, Christ might be visualized as the important cornice at the very top of the entire structure, the ornate attraction that adds its own beauty to the building. How excellently the apostle portrays the Lord Jesus as the beginning and the climax of all that pertains to His Church: its history, structure, doctrine, faith, and hope. The Lord is the sum of all the substance that is fitly joined together to form a holy temple in the Lord, that achievement that will be the eternal habitation of God (Ephesians 2:21-22).

The Head of the Church

It is of the risen and glorified Lord that the apostle writes to the Ephesians: God "hath put all things under His feet, and gave Him to be the head over all things to the church, which is His body, the fullness of Him that filleth all in all" (Ephesians 1:22-23). Here we have a dual concept: first, Christ transcendent in absolute authority; in the second place, Christ in organic union with His own. The first suggests submission to Christ; the second, union with Christ.

"But now we see not yet all things put under Him. But we see Jesus, who was made a little [for a little time] lower than the angels for the suffering of death, crowned with glory and honour" (Hebrews 2:8-9). "Wherefore God also hath highly exalted Him, and given Him a name which is above every name: that at the name of Jesus every knee should bow, of things in heaven, and things in earth, and things under the earth; and that every tongue should confess that Jesus Christ is Lord, to the glory of God the Father" (Philippians 2:9-11).

Obviously there were some in the Church at Colosse who had deviated so far from reality that they were worshiping angelic principalities over which the Father had made the Son supreme. They were not holding the Head (Colossians 2:18-19); consequently they were guilty of insubordination. They were not giving to Christ the place that was rightly His, solely and supremely above all.

"Let no man beguile you of your reward," counseled the apostle. To be defrauded of a prize or a reward is to suffer loss. There are other grave issues, perhaps not as serious as those at Colosse, which may deprive a local congregation of the enjoyment of riches in Christ.

Moreover, there is a link of life between the Head and the

Body and among all the members of that one Body: "For as the body is one, and hath many members, and all the members of that one body, being many, are one body: so also is Christ" (1 Corinthians 12:12).

This union is indissoluble and eternal. Therefore every member "should have the same care one for another. And whether one member suffer, all the members suffer with it; or one member be honoured, all the members rejoice with it" (1 Corinthians 12:25-26).

Christ is the Head of the Body, the Church, He is the Beginning, the Firstborn from the dead, that in all things He might have the preeminence.

The Great Shepherd

The Prophet Isaiah has graphically described the sinner's position and condition in the world: "All we like sheep have gone astray; we have turned every one to his own way" (Isaiah 53:6). Happy are they of whom the words of Peter are true: "Ye were as sheep going astray; but are now returned to the Shepherd and [Overseer] of your souls" (1 Peter 2:25). They can now honestly say, "The Lord is my Shepherd" (Psalm 23:1).

The shepherd and the various activities of the shepherd occupy a prominent place in patriarchal history. The care that those men exercised in tending their flocks is used in the Word of God to illustrate the need of God's people and the attention that their nature and condition demands. The fact that King David, the man after God's own heart, was a shepherd indicates that the Lord in His choice of David supplied the pastoral care and help that His people required.

The idea of the shepherd and his sheep readily passes from the Old Testament into the New. It is there, in the New, that we learn that the Lord Jesus Himself is the Shepherd and Overseer of souls. He no longer has a fold—His flock is much too large—yet that flock has but one Shepherd. He said, "Other sheep I have, which are not of this fold: them also I must bring, and they shall hear My voice; and there shall be one flock, one shepherd" (John 10:16 R.V.).

He is the good Shepherd who gave His life to save His sheep, and He still goes on giving His life for His sheep. "He tends with sweet unwearied care the flock for which He died."

The benediction with which the Epistle to the Hebrews closes indicates the deep concern that God has for His children, and the place that the Great Shepherd occupies in the perfecting and the uniting of the one flock: "Now the God of peace, that brought again from the dead our Lord Jesus, that great shepherd of the sheep, through the blood of the everlasting covenant, make you perfect in every good work to do His will, working in you that which is well-pleasing in His sight, through Jesus Christ; to whom be glory for ever and ever. Amen" (Hebrews 13:20-21).

Such is the solicitude of the Great Shepherd for His sheep that He delegates some as undershepherds "to feed the flock of God" allotted to them, and when all such shepherd ministry is finished, He as the Chief, the Head Shepherd, will distribute the recompenses. He shall appear, for "He that shall come will come, and will not tarry" (Hebrews 10:37). Then shall the undershepherds receive a crown of glory that never fades (1 Peter 5:1-4).

The Great High Priest

Priesthood in the Bible reaches back as far as Cain and Abel. Every man in those early, early days was prepared for priestly service. In patriarchal times this ministry was performed by the head of the family. Job, Abraham, Jacob, and Isaac all engaged in priestly functions for their families.

In Israel the Lord commanded, "Ye shall be unto Me a

kingdom of priests, and an holy nation'' (Exodus 19:6), but in this as in so much else, the nation failed. Eventually God made choice of Aaron to be the priest for His people. The Lord said, ''I will sanctify the tabernacle of the congregation, and the altar; I will sanctify also both Aaron and his sons, to minister to Me in the priest's office'' (Exodus 29:44).

In this church era, of course, we enjoy the priesthood of all believers. The Apostle Peter instructs us, ''Ye also as [living] stones are built up a spiritual house, an holy priesthood. . . . Ye are a chosen generation, a royal priesthood'' (1 Peter 2:5,9). As has been said, ''God's people today are a holy priesthood in character and a royal priesthood in dignity.''

The functions of a priest are both Godward and manward. He represents God to man and man to God.

The Divine Priest

With this Biblical outline of priesthood on the human level, let us consider the Lord Jesus, our Great High Priest. There were many priests in Israel, but there is only one who is worthy of the appellation, Great High Priest. The sum of all that has been written, and all that may now be said, is, ''We have such an high priest, who is set on the right hand of the throne of the Majesty in the heavens'' (Hebrews 8:1). ''We have a great high priest, who is passed into the heavens, Jesus the Son of God'' (Hebrews 4:14). Furthermore, He is ''a merciful and faithful high priest in things pertaining to God'' (Hebrews 2:17).

As our Great High Priest, He feels with us in our infirmities, our frailties. He has compassion on the ignorant, and He is able also to succor them that are tempted.

''This man,'' says the author of the Epistle to the Hebrews, ''because He continueth ever, hath an unchangeable priesthood. Wherefore He is able also to save them to the uttermost that come unto God by Him" (Hebrews 7:24-25). This He does because "He ever liveth to make intercession for them."

> This is not to be conceived of either as an external and vocal petitioning, nor as a mere figure of speech for the natural and continuous influence of His sacrifice; but rather as a special activity of Christ in securing, upon the ground of that sacrifice, whatever of blessing comes to men, whether that blessing be temporal or spiritual.[1]

The Advocate

Our Lord was the first Comforter that His disciples knew. When He left them He sent another Comforter (another of the same type as the first one), the Holy Spirit. Notwithstanding, the Lord Jesus at God's right hand is still a Comforter for His people. The word Comforter and the word Advocate in the original are the same. What a comfort to have an Advocate to represent us before the Father.

The Apostle John wrote, "My little children, these things write I unto you, that ye sin not." Here is the perfect standard at which all believers should aim, but, because of the Adamic nature that they still have, they cannot reach. John encourages all such by making mention of the provision for possible sin. "We have an Advocate with the Father, Jesus Christ the righteous" (1 John 2:1). An advocate is one who speaks on behalf of another in a court of law. What a picture of the blessed Lord Jesus.

The Priest Who Offers

There is another function that the Lord performs for His people. The exhortation is given, "By Him therefore let us offer the sacrifice of praise to God continually, that is, the

---

[1]A. H. Strong, *Systematic Theology,* page 775.

fruit of our lips giving thanks to His name'' (Hebrews 13:15).

Through their high priest Israel offered sweet incense upon the golden altar; believers of the Church period may offer spiritual sacrifices to God by Jesus Christ.

Much incense is ascending
  Before the eternal throne;
God graciously is bending
  To hear each feeble groan.
To all our prayers and praises
  Christ adds His sweet perfume,
And love the censer raises
  Their odors to consume.

Such then is the present ministry of the Lord Jesus in the heavens. He sustains His own in spite of their weaknesses; He makes constant intercession for them in their needs and in the presence of God; when they sin, He is their Advocate.

Righteous—as our Advocate, Christ is not a mere suppliant petitioner. He pleads for us on the grounds of justice, of righteousness, of obedience to the law, and endurance of its full penalty for us, on which He grounds His claim for our acquittal. The sense therefore is, ''in that He is righteous,'' in contrast to our sin (if any man sin). The Father, by raising Him from the dead and setting Him at His own right hand, has once for all accepted Christ's claim for us. Therefore the accuser's charges against God's children are vain. ''The righteousness of Christ stands on our side, for God's righteousness is, in Jesus Christ, ours.''[1]

A Ministry on Earth

When Israel fought with Amalek in the wilderness (Exodus 17:8-16), Moses ascended the mount and there strengthened Israel's fighting men by his action. Joshua in the plain below

---

[1]Jamieson, Fausset, and Brown, *Commentary, New Testament,* page 527.

also helped Israel; he went and fought against the enemy. Here we have a dual illustration of the Lord Jesus. He has ascended on high, and from there ministers to His struggling saints. At the same time He is here with them. The Apostle Paul in writing to the Romans argues, "Since Christ be in you" certain development must take place. Christ is in the believer. In writing to the Colossians, the same apostle avers, "this mystery . . . which is Christ in you, the hope of glory" (Colossians 1:27). The indwelling Christ is to God's children like the glory and dawn of the eternal day. May He be this to all. May He in this positive manner defeat for us the foe.

Bodily our Lord is in heaven but because of His omnipresence He spiritually can still be with His own on earth.

The analogy of the vine and its branches (John 15) may also indicate another aspect of His present ministry on earth. He provides the life and vigor to those who abide in Him. Through this provision they may bear fruit while living in this poor world. Said our Lord to His disciples, "Herein is My Father glorified, that ye bear much fruit; so shall ye be My disciples" (John 15:8).

> God is said to have been glorified in the work of the Son. Now we have the other truth that God is glorified in the work of believers who abide in the Son. There is an air of completeness and of certainty about it. The disciples will surely glorify the Father by their continual fruit-bearing.[1]

The Forerunner

"A forerunner," says Dr. Merrill Unger, "is used in the sense of one who comes in advance to a place whither the rest are to follow."[2]

---

[1]Leon Morris, Gospel of John, in *New International Commentary,* page 672.

[2]*Unger's Bible Dictionary,* Chicago, Moody Press, page 377.

In His own language the Lord Jesus so pictures Himself: "If I go and prepare a place for you, I will come again, and receive you unto Myself; that where I am there ye may be also" (John 14:3).

Speaking of our hope, the Epistle to the Hebrews says, "Which hope we have as an anchor of the soul, both sure and stedfast, and which entereth . . . within the veil; whither the Forerunner is for us entered, even Jesus, made an high priest for ever after the order of Melchisedec" (Hebrews 6:19-20).

The term forerunner in this context may be considered a nautical term. There are several of these terms scattered throughout the Epistle. Their use confirms the contention of some that this remarkable treatise, which very few doubt contains the material of the Apostle Paul, was written by one of his traveling companions who had imbibed, on their journeys, the language of the sailors.

Until highways were built and trailer-tractors began carrying goods along the Caribbean coastline, small sailing ships used to move quite large cargoes of freight. Occasionally, as these approached a harbor there would not be sufficient breeze by which to enter. The crew would lower a small boat with a line attached and it would be rowed to the mooring dock. Once there, by the line a heavy cable would be pulled ashore and firmly anchored. The crew aboard the cargo ship would then hand-over-hand literally pull their vessel into its moorings and there make it secure.

The small boat was the forerunner; its safe arrival was the assurance of the safe arrival of the larger ship. Even so is it with the Lord Jesus our Forerunner and Anchor. He has entered within the veil. His presence there assures that where He is, there shall we be also.

As John the Baptist was Christ's forerunner to announce His coming, so Christ is our Forerunner to prepare for our coming.

The Bridegroom

In retrospect, the relationship into which all believers were brought to Christ at Pentecost is expressed in the analogy of the body. During the present this relationship is seen in the building, the Church. Eventually, beyond the rapture the eternal and intimate union between Christ and His Church will be manifest in the relationship of Bridegroom and bride.

That Christ the Bridegroom has long anticipated the joy of this eternal oneness is set forth in His promises, His attitude, His succor, and His support for all the saints during this era of grace.

In the past. "Christ also loved the church, and gave Himself for it" (Ephesians 5:25-27). So great is His love that He gave Himself up, He surrendered Himself, to all the indignities, anguish, and agony from which He might have delivered Himself by the exercise of His divine prerogatives.

> 'Twas love that held Him to the tree
> Or iron could ne'r have bound Him.

Each member of His Church individually may say, "The life which I now live in the flesh I live by the faith of the Son of God, who loved me, and gave Himself for me" (Galatians 2:20). On Calvary the Lord Jesus was the perfect substitute for the believer.

To the small nucleus from which the Church developed, the Lord Jesus said, "I go to prepare a place for you. And if I go and prepare a place for you, I will come again, and receive you unto Myself; that where I am, there ye may be also" (John 14:23).

That the prepared place is inside the veil seems clear from a comparison of Scripture. The veil that shut man out from God was rent when the Saviour died (Matthew 27:51). Now a new and living way has been consecrated through the veil (Hebrews 10:20).

In the present. Christ gave Himself up, "That He might sanctify and cleanse it [the Church] with the washing of water by the word" (Ephesians 5:26). There are some who consider this as an initial experience in the life of each member of the Church. In writing to the Corinthians, the apostle said, "Such were some of you [immoral]: but ye are washed, but ye are sanctified . . . in the name of the Lord Jesus, and by the Spirit of our God" (1 Corinthians 6:11), and this certainly was initial.

That such a necessary experience is required is clear, but is such the meaning of the Ephesian passage? May it not be teaching a process rather than an event, the process of preparing the bride? Perhaps the preparation of Esther for her marriage to Ahasuerus provides an example, though a rather poor one. Water in this passage is a symbol of the Word of God. The constant cleansing properties of pure water indicate the need and value of daily washings. The Lord Jesus prayed the Father for His own: "Sanctify them through Thy truth: Thy Word is truth" (John 17:17).

> The sanctification that Jesus looks for the Father to accomplish will be worked in their doing the truth. . . . Sanctification is not effective apart from the divine revelation.[1]

"Heaven is a prepared place for a prepared people," wrote Dr. A. C. Gaebelein many years ago.

The future. There are two specific portions of the New Testament which must be examined to acquire any knowledge of the glorious future of the Church as a bride: the passage to which reference has been made in the Epistle to the Ephesians and the other from Revelation.

The objective before the Lord in regard to His Church has always been "that He might present it to Himself a glorious

---

[1]Leon Morris, Gospel of John, *New International Commentary,* page 730.

church'' (Ephesians 5:27). The Apostle Paul said to the people of God at Corinth, which statement would include all the Church: ''I am jealous over you with godly jealousy: for I have espoused you to one husband, that I may present you as a chaste virgin to Christ'' (2 Corinthians 11:2). Now that chaste virgin is fully prepared to be presented by Christ Himself to Himself a glorious Church. ''Holiness is glory internally; glory is holiness shining outwardly.''

The perfect state of the Church is magnificent. She is ''without spot,'' for there is no moral defilement; ''without wrinkle,'' for there is no physical deterioration; or ''any such thing,'' for there is no general degeneracy. She is absolutely pure and perfect.

The marriage of the Lamb and the marriage supper of the Lamb are mentioned separately (Revelation 19:7-9) as if they are two different events. The suggestion made by some may be correct, that the marriage itself takes place in Heaven, whereas the marriage supper takes place on earth to facilitate the attendance of ''the friend of the bridegroom'' (John 3:29), and all who are invited.

Just exactly when in the divine program the marriage supper will be enjoyed is difficult to say. There is little value in conjectures; nevertheless the suggestion may have some merit that the marriage supper will follow the resurrection of Old Testament saints and saints from the great tribulation period (Daniel 12:1-3; Revelation 20:4).

''Alleluia: for the Lord God omnipotent reigneth. Let us be glad and rejoice, and give honour to Him: for the marriage of the Lamb is come, and His wife hath made herself ready'' (Revelation 19:6-7). The wedding gown, so the passage states, is of fine linen which ''is the righteousness of saints.''

Two different interpretations have been circulated of ''the righteousness of saints.'' Both are based on the plurality of the word righteousness in the text. It could properly read, "the righteousnesses of the saints." Some therefore assume that it refers to the righteous acts performed in life by the saints. These will there, so it is claimed, be seen to their credit.

The second interpretation, originated by C. H. Spurgeon, is that the plurality here, like similar construction elsewhere, means the bounteous and generous provision of the righteousness of Christ imputed to the believer.

Isaiah speaks of "the wells of salvation" out of which many will drink in glorious millennial days (Isaiah 12:3). He also describes the King in Righteousness who will be as "rivers of water in a dry place" (Isaiah 32:1-2). Wells, waters—ample provision indeed.

This writer, although taught the first interpretation as a young believer, finds himself partial to the second. On that superlative occasion we shall not appear in anything that we have done, but wholly and solely in the perfect redundant righteousness of Christ.

10

THE MORNING STAR

Christians in general believe in the coming again of the Lord Jesus. This is the hope of the entire Christian Church. The great diversity of opinion among Christians arises from belief or disbelief in either the millennium or the great tribulation. Some believe in neither and are considered amillenarians.

Unfortunately even millenarians are not of one accord in this important matter. They differ much among themselves. There are those who believe that the Church will go through the great tribulation, after which the Lord will come. Another minority group feels that Christ will return in the middle of the great tribulation; that is, in the middle of Daniel's seventieth week.

There is a firm belief on the part of many that the Lord will fulfill His promise previous to the tribulation period, therefore previous to the millennium.

A Literal Interpretation

A study of these future events is influenced by one's own attitude. If the Scriptures are to be interpreted allegorically the literal predictions concerning the restoration of Israel to divine favor may easily be accepted as being but figures of blessings for the Church, thus depriving the Hebrew nation of the benefits of the Abrahamic and Davidic covenants. The distinction between God's full grace among the nations and His plan for Israel was stated by James at the first council of the Church in Jerusalem: "After this [that is, the Church era, the day of salvation among all nations] I will return, and will build again the tabernacle of David, which is fallen down; and I will build again the ruins thereof, and will set it up" (Acts 15:5-16). That first council had a keen appreciation of the difference between Israel and the Church.

A close examination of the Holy Scriptures and a literal interpretation of applicable passages will result in the conviction that there is a great tribulation and a glorious millennium in future for this world. During the great tribulation the Jewish nation particularly will suffer, but that grievous period will be followed by the reign of the Lord Jesus in absolute righteousness. He shall then be King of kings and Lord of lords.

Of Deep Concern

The Apostle John in his vision on Patmos saw a great multitude arrayed in white robes. A question arose about that multitude: "Whence came they?" and the answer was given, "These are they which came out of great tribulation, [the tribulation, the great one, *The Englishman's Greek New Testament*], and have washed their robes, and made them white in the blood of the Lamb" (Revelation 7:13-14). It is important that we notice the Holy Spirit uses the definite article to designate the tribulation from which these have emerged. It is the great tribulation.

The Prophet Daniel records a description of that dreadful time. He also includes a promise to the Hebrew nation: "And there shall be a time of trouble, such as never was since there was a nation even to that same time: and at that time thy people shall be delivered, every one that shall be found written in the book" (Daniel 12:1).

On one occasion the Lord Jesus sat on the Mount of Olives and talked to His disciples of eschatological events. He gave a similar description to Daniel's: "Then shall be great tribulation, such as was not since the beginning of the world to this time, no, nor ever shall be. And except those days should be shortened, there should no flesh be saved, but for the elect's sake those days shall be shortened" (Matthew 24:21-22).

In view of the descriptive words of Christ, it would seem that Paul had this uttermost suffering in mind when he wrote to the saints at Thessalonica, and mentioned God's punitive wrath against the anti-Christian hatred of the Jews toward the children of God. "For ye, brethren, became followers of the churches of God which in Judea are in Christ Jesus: for ye also have suffered like things of your own countrymen, even as they have of the Jews: Who both killed the Lord Jesus, and their own prophets, and have persecuted us; and they please not God, and are contrary to all men: Forbidding us to speak to the Gentiles that they might be saved, to fill up their sins alway: for the wrath is come upon them to the uttermost" (1 Thessalonians 2:14-16).

There can be no reasonable doubt concerning these descriptions. An incomparable, unparalleled time of suffering is predicated in all. The further details given by the Lord only make the whole dreadful matter more evident.

Will the Church go through this unsurpassed time of tribulation? That the Church has suffered much tribulation ever since Pentecost is well recorded in history. The apostle wrote to his young Thessalonian converts: "That no man should be moved by these afflictions: for yourselves know that ye are appointed thereunto. For verily, when we were with you, we told you before that we should suffer tribulation; even as it came to pass, and ye know" (1 Thessalonians 3:3-4). Notwithstanding, there has been no worldwide trouble such as described by Daniel and by the Lord.

The assurance of salvation from the great tribulation is embodied in the gospel, in one of the "much more's" of

Romans 5:9: "Much more then, being now justified by His blood [a completed act], we shall be saved from wrath through Him." Wrath here is abstract; it therefore intimates any kind of wrath. The believer through Christ is delivered from all aspects of wrath, even the great tribulation.

The Lord Himself was revealed to the Thessalonians, and to us, as the Deliverer from future wrath. *The New Testament in Current English* by Ferrar Fenton reads: "His Son from heaven, whom He raised from the dead—Jesus, our Deliverer from the terror of the future" (1 Thessalonians 1:10).

That there is an extension of the work of salvation in the future is clear. It is by divine appointment, and is implied in Paul's further statement to the Thessalonians: "For God hath not appointed us to wrath, but to obtain salvation by our Lord Jesus Christ" (1 Thessalonians 5:9-10). One cannot fail to see the application here to the great tribulation.

In His letter to the Church at Philadelphia the Lord speaks of a "temptation which shall come upon all the world, to try them that dwell upon the earth" (Revelation 3:10). If the above assumption is correct, here is a promise to the Church that she will be kept out of the great tribulation.

His Promised Return

While the return of the Lord is scripturally one event, it will be accomplished in two phases; first He comes as the Bright and Morning Star for His Church, and then as the Root and Offspring of David to Israel. These specific titles are taken from the book of the Revelation: "I Jesus have sent Mine angel to testify unto you these things in the churches. I am the root and the offspring of David, and the bright and morning star" (Revelation 22:16).

In delineating the actual rapture of the Church, the apostle uses a verb that contributes to an understanding of that event: "We which are alive and remain shall be caught up together with them [the dead in Christ] in the clouds, to meet the Lord in the air" (1 Thessalonians 4:17).

The verb meet intimates a going forth to make contact with a person and to have that person return with you to the point of starting. At the rapture, the Church will be caught away to meet the Lord in the air in order to return with Him to earth.

Four Distinctive Days

There are four special periods of time mentioned in the New Testament. To know their significance is to have the key to many prophetic subjects.

Man's day. The Apostle Paul resented the criticism of the Corinthians: "With me it is a very small thing that I should be judged of you, or of man's judgment [man's day, marginal reading]: yea, I judge not mine own self" (1 Corinthians 4:3).

Some have equated man's day with "the times of the Gentiles." The time of the Gentiles began with Nebuchadnezzar and the captivity of Judah. No one in those times could ever have expressed a personal, public opinion against another. Nebuchadnezzar was a monarch in the absolute sense of the word. Man's day, the day of popular opinion, probably started with the Roman democracy. This special feature of man's day is quite characteristic of modern times.

Man's day will end shortly after the rapture of the Church, for another, more powerful than Nebuchadnezzar, will arise and public opinions will cease.

The Day of Christ. This span of a few years is mentioned only by the Apostle Paul. He hoped and no doubt prayed that the Corinthians might "be blameless in the day of our Lord Jesus Christ" (1 Corinthians 1:8). In writing to the Philippians, he said, "That ye may approve things that are excellent; that ye may be sincere and without offence till the day of Christ'' (Philippians 1:10).

In all the references to the day of Christ there is a hint of a future examination of the believer and his conduct.

The day of Christ always has to do with the Church, and with the Church in the heavens with her Lord. Bible students have concluded that the day of Christ begins with the rapture of the Church and is characterized by the judgment seat of Christ and the marriage of the Lamb. It ends with the descent of Christ and His bride to the earth.

The Day of the Lord. This day is mentioned in both the Old Testament and the New. There is a reference to it in some marginal readings of 2 Thessalonians 2:2: ''That ye be not soon shaken in mind, or be troubled, neither by spirit, nor by word, nor by letter as from us, as that the day of the Lord has come.''

In the Old Testament it is called ''the day of vengeance of our God'' (Isaiah 61:2). Some of its special features are given by Zechariah and Isaiah in numerous passages.

The day of the Lord in contrast to the day of Christ always is related to things on earth. It begins shortly after the rapture of the Church with the ascendancy of the beast of Rome, the future dictator over the European community of nations.

The day of the Lord is a prolonged period probably stretching to the end of time. It includes Daniel's seventieth week, the millennium, the final satanic and human revolt against God and His saints. Some believe that the great white throne judgment may be the last act of the day of the Lord.

The Day of God. This is mentioned but once in the Scriptures. It is God's eternity with a new Heaven and a new earth (2 Peter 3:12).

The Judgment Seat

Particular attention should be paid to the details of the day of Christ. If this is done, it will be observed that the event to follow the rapture is the judgment seat of Christ. For the Christian this is a very important matter.

The believer should constantly remember the argument of the Apostle Peter, "If [since] ye call on the Father, who without respect of persons judgeth according to every man's work, pass the time of your sojourning here in fear" (1 Peter 1:17). The heavenly Father is constantly assessing the lives of His children. A spiritual awareness of this should not result in slavish fear, but in holy reverence. There is a sense in which we are always in God's presence and His eye is ever upon us; our behavior therefore should be in perfect accord with His nearness. Notwithstanding this constant assessment of character and conduct there will be a close examination of all the believer has been and has done. This will be at the judgment seat of Christ.

The significant features of this event are dealt with in three major passages of the New Testament. From these it is learned that all believers must stand before that judgment seat (Romans 14:7-13; 1 Corinthians 3:12-15; 2 Corinthians 5:9-11).

The solemnity of the Judgment Seat. A forceful evidence of the solemnity of this occasion is seen in the Old Testament quotation used by the apostle in teaching this subject: "We shall all stand before the judgment seat of Christ. For it is written, As I live, saith the Lord, every knee shall bow to Me, and every tongue shall confess to God. So then every one of us shall give account of himself to God" (Romans 14:10-12). One is not surprised that certain Biblical authorities make Paul's statement to read, "For we must all appear before *the judgment seat of God.*"

It has been averred that the Greek word *bema* translated in this passage "judgment seat" is equivalent to a modern umpire's box in the world of sports. Such a description is very inadequate. The word was used in sports, but it was also used in Roman military services. A commander would stand upon the raised platform, the bema, and brief his soldiers before a battle. When victorious, from the same bema he would compliment them. Pilate sat upon a bema, a judgment seat at the trial of the Lord Jesus Christ; that was a very solemn matter (Matthew 27:19).

The judgment seat of Christ will be a solemn review of the Christian's life, from its beginning to its close.

The purpose of the Judgment Seat. Sin and its penalty are not charges to be laid before this judgment seat. The believer's sins have all been atoned for: "There is therefore now no condemnation [no judgment] to them which are in Christ Jesus" (Romans 8:1).

The life of each believer in Christ is to be examined but not with any penalty in view. The three major passages already mentioned intimate different aspects of Christian conduct. First, the believer's attitude toward others will be scrutinized: "So then every one of us shall give account of himself to God. Let us not therefore judge one another any more: but judge this rather, that no man put a stumblingblock or an occasion to fall in his brother's way" (Romans 14:12-13).

In the second place, there will be a specific appraisal of the Christian's service: "Every man's work shall be made manifest: for the day shall declare it, because it shall be revealed by fire; and the fire shall try every man's work of what sort it is" (1 Corinthians 3:13).

> Underlying this passage is the thought of the Christian life as the erection of a building the foundation of which has already been laid. With the laying of the foundation we ourselves have nothing to do. That is a work that was completed nearly two thousand years ago. With the character of the building we erect on this foundation, however, we have a great deal to do. It is for us to say whether it will be built of that which may be likened to wood, hay, and

stubble; or to that which may be likened to gold, silver, and costly stones. The passage makes clear, moreover, that these lives of ours will one day be subjected to a test that will distinguish as unerringly between the good and the bad in them as fire is able to distinguish between what is built of wood, hay, and stubble and what is built of gold, silver, and costly stone. Also that the reward meted out to us on that day will be strictly in proportion to the good found in our lives.[1]

Finally, in writing to the same Corinthians, Paul tells of a complete inquiry into the actions of life: "For we must all appear before the judgment seat of Christ; that every one may receive the things done in his body, according to that he hath done, whether it be good or bad" (2 Corinthians 5:10). Not bad, in the sense of sinful, but that the activities of the Christian's life may be worthwhile or worthless.

The results at the Judgment Seat. The state of all members of the Church after the rapture will be that of absolute perfection: "Beloved, now are we the sons of God, and it doth not appear what we shall be: but we know that, when He shall appear, we shall be like Him; for we shall see Him as He is" (1 John 3:2). Consequently there will be complete accord between the Judge and those who stand before Him. Even in suffering loss, there will be relief and joy in the final destruction of the "wood, hay, and stubble of life," that which is indeed worthless in every respect.

How very terse the decision: "If any man's work abide which he hath built thereupon, he shall receive a reward. If any man's work shall be burned, he shall suffer loss: but he himself shall be saved; yet so as by fire" (1 Corinthians 3:13-15). Some will forfeit the special award that might have been theirs, but with no loss of that eternal life which was a

---

[1]Samuel G. Craig, *Jesus of Yesterday and Today,* Philadelphia, Presbyterian and Reformed, page 168.

free gift to them: "For by grace are ye saved through faith" (Ephesians 2:8).

As a builder whose building was consumed would escape with personal safety, but with the loss of his work.[1]

As the shipwrecked merchant, though he lose all his merchandise, is saved, even although having to pass through the waves.[2]

As gold and silver in the crucible passing through the assayer's furnace are both preserved and purified, even so will all the Lord's own be saved at the Judgment Seat.

Rewards

The Lord Jesus, speaking pictorially, tells of a wealthy man who interrogated his servants as to how they had occupied themselves during his prolonged absence. To some he said, "Well done, thou good and faithful servant: thou hast been faithful over a few things. I will make thee ruler over many things" (Matthew 25:21). Here the course is plotted, examined, commended, and recompensed.

Some, possibly all, will suffer some loss, for the Word of God states: "The Lord . . . who both will bring to light the hidden things of darkness, and will make manifest the counsels of the hearts: and then shall every man have [his own due] praise of God" (1 Corinthians 4:5).

For the believer in this age of grace there are rewards which are likened to crowns, stephanos crowns. The stephanos crown was woven of evergreen branches and was awarded in ancient times to the winner of a sport contest. It should not be confused with the diadem, the crown of kings. It is predicted of our Lord Jesus, "On His head were many crowns [many diadems]" (Revelation 19:12).

---

[1]Henry Alford, *The New Testament for English Readers,* page 992.

[2]Bengel, quoted by Jamieson, Fausset, and Brown. page 268.

An incorruptible crown. This is the symbol of the reward granted to the man who is able to master himself, to keep his body under control. "They [contestants in the world] do it to obtain a corruptible crown; but we [Christian athletes in training] an incorruptible" (1 Corinthians 9:25).

Converts won to Christ in life will form *a crown of rejoicing* for every soul winner: "For what is our hope, or joy, or crown of rejoicing?" wrote the apostle to the Thessalonians. "Are not even ye in the presence of our Lord Jesus Christ at His coming? For ye are our glory and joy" (1 Thessalonians 2:19-20).

Soon the Lord will fulfill His promise, "I will come again." To them who with eager suspense await that great day, there is this promise, "Henceforth there is laid up for me a crown of righteousness, which the Lord, the righteous judge, shall give me at that day: and not to me only, but unto all them also that love His appearing" (2 Timothy 4:8).

To the severely tried and to those who are faithful to the Lord irrespective of even the severity of martyrdom, there will be given *the crown of life.* "Blessed is the man that endureth temptation [trial]: for when he is tried, he shall receive the crown of life, which the Lord hath promised to them that love Him" (James 1:12). "Be thou faithful unto death, and I will give thee a crown of life" (Revelation 2:10).

Since postpentecostal times thousands of God's people have won the martyr's crown. Even in this modern age of indifference both paganism and communism have extended the long list of martyrs.

Like their Master there are those who as good shepherds daily are giving their lives for the sheep. "When the chief Shepherd shall appear, ye shall receive *a crown of glory* that fadeth not away" (1 Peter 5:4).

In this period of time characterized by apathy, compromise, and infidelity in the world and in the Church, a clarion call in the Saviour's own words needs to be raised: "Behold, I come quickly: hold that fast which thou hast, that no man take thy crown" (Revelation 3:11). What an incentive to Christian living and service!

"Behold I Come"

"To receive to Myself." "If I go and prepare a place for you, I will come again, and receive you unto Myself" (John 14:1-4).

The disciples were perplexed, for the Lord's announcement that He was leaving them, and that they could not go with Him, had more than surprised them. Furthermore, the Lord's rebuke to Peter's boastful claim of faithfulness and courage had left them all shamed and silenced.

Into the perturbed hearts of these crestfallen men, as a veritable balm of grace was poured the promise of the personal return of the Lord. A paraphrasing of His meaning might help in making His message clearer: I am going away, and shall no longer be with you here in this sphere of trouble, sorrow, and death; but I am coming again to receive you to Myself so that you will be with Me there in a sphere of life, peace, and joy.

Throughout all the centuries of the Christian Church no other words, either written or spoken, have so consoled and reanimated the dismayed and discouraged hearts of God's people. The Lord's promise personally to return for His own, and the assurance of its fulfillment, has quieted many laments, soothed much anguish, rekindled hope, and revitalized the life of myriads of grief-stricken and dejected saints.

On other occasions the disciples had heard the Lord speak rather figuratively about the temple as "His Father's house." The Jews had made "His Father's house" a center of merchandise. Twice over the Lord had expelled such affronts from its courts, but now He is using its structure illustratively.

In the original temple were three stories of apartments, called chambers (1 Kings 6:5-7), so in the Father's house above there are also many places of abode. In the King James Version these are called mansions. Could these be the heavenly dwelling places of celestial beings, principalities, and powers? Our Lord went to prepare a special place for His Church; He went by way of Calvary. There the entrance was penetrated. When the Lord Jesus cried, "It is finished," "the veil of the temple was rent in twain from the top to the bottom" (Matthew 27:51). "Having therefore, brethren, boldness to enter into the holiest by the blood of Jesus, By a new and living way, which He hath consecrated for us, through the veil, that is to say, His flesh" (Hebrews 10:19-20).

The prepared place is inside the veil. There we now may enter in spirit, but after His return the Church shall be forever with Him.

Through Thy precious body broken
    Inside the veil;
O what words to sinners spoken
    Inside the veil!
Precious as the blood that bought us,
Perfect as the love that sought us,
Holy as the Lamb that brought us
    Inside the veil.

Soon Thy saints shall all be gathered
    Inside the veil:
All at home, no more be scattered,
    Inside the veil.
Nought from Thee our hearts shall sever;
We shall see Thee, grieve Thee never;

"Praise the Lamb!" shall sound forever
Inside the veil.

ELIZABETH DARK

"Caught up together." This is the hope of the Christian Church. What an expectation, to be caught up (to be raptured away) to meet the Lord in the air!

There had been distress among the young Christians in Thessalonica. Some of their fellow believers had died; in fact, some may have been martyred, and the assembly was disquieted. There were those who mourned not only the passing home of their loved ones, their loss, but because of ignorance they thought that the dead in Christ would not participate in the rapture of the Church. The apostle wrote patiently instructing them again, "We told you before that we should suffer tribulation; even as it came to pass" (1 Thessalonians 3:4). He then very considerately explained how the rapture will take place, and how both the dead in Christ and the living will be "caught up together" to meet the Lord in the air.

The Church today is waiting momentarily for the consummation of that bright hope. At the same time she knows that logically such can take place only when there is a resurrection.

The Resurrection

It is little wonder that the Jewish people sought to kill the Lord Jesus. Over and above His claims of equality with God the Father (John 10:29-33) He certainly claimed supernatural powers. Speaking of each one who believes in Him, the Saviour asserts, he "may have everlasting life: and I will raise him up at the last day" (John 6:10). If Jesus were merely a man, merely human, such claims would be preposterous. Such are His prerogatives that Christ declared that He would even perform the resurrection (John 6:39-40).

The people of God throughout all generations in both Old

and New Testament times have believed in a resurrection. Job, probably living in the days of Abraham, was very bold in stating his convictions: ''Though after my skin worms destroy this body, yet in my flesh shall I see God: Whom I shall see for myself, and mine eyes shall behold, and not another [not a stranger]; though my reins be consumed within me'' (Job 19:26-27).

The Apostle Paul not only believed in the resurrection himself, he taught it. He has given numerous details regarding this event in his letter to the Corinthians, and the imagery is fascinating: ''As in Adam all die, even so in Christ shall all be made alive. But every man in his own order [his own rank]'' (1 Corinthians 15:23). Jamieson, Fausset, and Brown in their commentary render this phrase concretely, ''Every man in his own regiment.'' The idea is that of a military parade with one regiment after another passing in review. Paul here pictures the first two regiments as they march past.

Our Lord Jesus in all must have the preeminence; therefore He is the Leader of this parade: ''Christ the firstfruits.'' Christ is ''the firstborn from the dead'' (Colossians 1:18). In His resurrection our Lord is the Firstfruits of a mighty harvest, the seeds of which have been planted throughout the ages. He is the Firstborn of the vast innumerable family of all who have died in Christ.

The second regiment in this auspicious parade is about to pass. It is composed of only ''they that are Christ's.'' As already noticed, these are the saints of the New Testament era, ''the dead in Christ.'' Let it be understood, these phrases indicate an intimate relationship to Christ; it is the unique relationship of Christ to the Church.

While other regiments are not individually mentioned here, they are not difficult to find in other passages of the Holy Scriptures.

Daniel, for example, describes the second half of that week of years known in prophecy as "Daniel's seventieth week," as "a time of trouble, such as never was since there was a nation even to that same time." There is only one comprehension of this text; taken literally it foretells the great tribulation. Since the interpretation of the text is based on the actual understanding of the language, to be consistent what follows must similarly be interpreted literally: "Many of them [Daniel's people] that sleep in the dust of the earth shall awake, some to everlasting life, and some to shame and everlasting contempt" (Daniel 12:2). It is not difficult to discern that this passage forms the background to our Lord's prediction, made to hateful Jews, of the resurrection (John 5:28-29).

May we not therefore conclude that the saints of the Old Testament, with probably the saints of the tribulation period, form the third regiment. The martyrs of that future time of unsurpassed suffering, who refuse to worship the beast or his image and refuse to receive his mark upon their foreheads or in their hands, will live and reign with Christ one thousand years. But the rest of the dead will not live again until the thousand years are finished.

The last regiment to be seen is indeed a doleful one. It follows the resurrection of life by one thousand years. It is the resurrection of damnation: "And I saw the dead, small and great, stand before God; and the books were opened: and another book was opened, which is the book of life: and the dead were judged out of those things which were written in the books, according to their works. And the sea gave up the dead which were in it; and death and hell delivered up the dead which were in them: and they were judged every man according to their works. . . . And whosoever was not found written in the book of life was cast into the lake of fire" (Revelation 20:12-15).

A Graphic Account

From this 1 Thessalonian 4 passage it will be observed that the Lord will return personally: "The Lord Himself shall descend from heaven." This is in perfect agreement with other related portions of the New Testament. The Apostle John records the Lord's own promise, "I will come again." The canon of Holy Scripture closes with the special announcement from the Lord Jesus Himself, "Surely, I come quickly."

The Lord will come with "a shout." A comment made by A. R. Fausset is very interesting: "In Greek, a single shout, a war shout. Jesus is represented as a victorious King giving the word of command to the hosts of Heaven in His train for the last onslaught, at His final triumph over sin, death, and Satan."

The Lord will come "with the voice of the archangel," who probably was commander over the celestial hosts. It may be that, like Lazarus who was carried by the angels into Abraham's bosom (Luke 16:19-22), the Church will have an angelic escort through hostile areas to the trysting place to meet her Lord. Her safety is altogether assured.

"With the trump of God." In writing to the Corinthians Paul calls this "the last trump." The last blast of Israel's silver trumpets was that which ushered in the year of jubilee (Numbers 10:10; Leviticus 25:9-13). It was sounded with the gladness of their hearts. This last trumpet was a befitting indication of the relief, rest, and joy in Israel's national experience after forty-nine years of toil and trouble.

The jubilee blast of the silver trumpets does not seem to fit very well into the rather militaristic context of the Thessalonian passage. To Roman soldiers the trumpet gave out the signals which expressed the orders of the commander. They were similar to the modern bugle. The first trumpet was to arouse all the sleeping troops; the second trumpet was the signal that all fall into rank; and the last trumpet issued the order to march away. It is for the last trump that the Church awaits.

The resurrection of the blessed dead, which we have already considered, is next mentioned in this apostolic delineation of the rapture.

Finally Paul adds, "Then we which are alive and remain shall be caught up together with them in clouds" (possibly in large groups which will cast cloud shadows on the earth as they ascend), "to meet the Lord in the air." Let the significance of the verb "to meet" be remembered. The Church will contact her Lord in the air in order that ultimately she will return to earth with Him (Revelation 19:11-16).

"Like Him." "Beloved, now are we the sons of God," this because of a reception given to the Lord Jesus. "As many as received Him, to them gave He power [the right] to become sons of God, even to them that believe on His name" (John 1:12). Furthermore, "It doth not yet appear what we shall be" (1 John 3:1-3). There is nothing about the lowly, mortal bodies of Christians that could even suggest what they shall be in the future, but we know that when He shall appear we shall be like Him. The Lord will be fully manifested in His own body of glory. The Lord Jesus will transform these perishable bodies and refashion them like unto His own body of glory. All believers then shall indeed be like Him. Moreover, "we shall see Him as He is."

We shall never see Him as He was in the humble guise, in the state of incognito, in which He appeared centuries ago in Palestine. We shall see Him then in His majestic glory. Just previous to His betrayal the Lord Jesus prayed, "Father, I will that they also, whom Thou hast given Me, be with Me where I am; that they may behold My glory, which Thou hast given Me: for Thou lovedst Me before the foundation of the world" (John 17:24).

When we thus see Him we shall know that the change has taken place, and that we are like Him. Before it could be possible that we look upon our now-glorified Lord, it would be necessary that we have the spiritual bodies of the resurrection. In our natural physical state we could never look upon that unsullied glory and splendor. A complete change from the fallen nature of Adam, both spiritual and physical, is required.

C. H. Spurgeon, whom we are told was a very humorous man, tried to explain this necessary complete transformation to his congregation: ''If a thief got into Heaven, he would still be a thief and probably would steal the money out of the angels' pockets.''

An elderly deacon, who was somewhat disgruntled by Mr. Spurgeon's outbursts of humor, waited on him one evening, and in reprimanding him, insisted that he apologize to the congregation.

On the first possible occasion, Mr. Spurgeon, a little irritated by the deacon's frequent criticisms, told his congregation of the visit from the deacon, and that he was asked to make a public apology. He also told them that the deacon had informed him that angels do not have pockets and that there is no money in circulation in Heaven. ''Notwithstanding,'' emphasized Mr. Spurgeon, ''I am convinced that if a thief got into Heaven he still would be a thief, and would steal the feathers out of the angels' wings.''

A complete spiritual and physical transfiguration is absolutely necessary for us to see our glorious Lord; that will certainly take place at the rapture of the Church: ''For this corruptible must put on incorruption, and this mortal must put on immortality'' (1 Corinthians 15:53).

The speaker at a large Christian convention announced his subject, The Second Advent of Christ. He then read a few excerpts from Revelation 22, and gave the outline of his sermon, which actually was on the triple promise of the Lord, "Behold, I come quickly." The Lord is coming to:

The Studious Steward. "Behold, I come quickly: Blessed is he that keepeth the sayings of this book" (verse 7).

The Sincere Servant. "Behold, I come quickly; and My reward is with Me, to give every man according as his work shall be" (verse 12).

The Suffering Saints. It was the imprisoned suffering saint John who responded: "Amen. Even so, come, Lord Jesus."

Following the regeneration of the universe, the bridal city, the Holy Jerusalem, descends from God. This is to be the home of the redeemed. It will be a beautiful and spacious city, so spotless in its purity that only those washed in the blood of the Lamb can enter it. In it will appear the "river of life," "the tree of life," and God Himself will be the light thereof.

Beyond the ages of turmoil and strife there will be the ushering in of eternal bliss. Harmony will be restored to the universe. Into the Father's house will be gathered the redeemed of the earth. Perfection and ineffable bliss will characterize moral beings.[1]

---

[1]P. B. Fitzwater, *Christian Theology*, page 547.

11
THE SUPREME SOVEREIGN

Divine, supreme sovereignty is a very extensive subject in the Holy Scriptures. David, a national king himself, understood this perfectly. He wrote, "The LORD hath prepared His throne in the heavens; and His kingdom ruleth over all" (Psalm 103:19). Asaph sang and surely with conviction, "That men may know that Thou, whose name alone is JEHOVAH, art the most high over all the earth" (Psalm 83:18).

The perfect rule of God over all His creation is developed throughout the Scriptures, progressively in history, prophecy, and in mystery. Divine sovereignty was in the past, is in the present, and evermore shall be.

In History

Frequently reference is made to the fixed laws of nature without much thought as to who created them and who controls them. Nature witnesses to her Creator. The elements perform according to His decree: "And God spake unto Noah, and to his sons with him . . . I do set My bow in the cloud, and it shall be for a token of a covenant between Me and the earth. And it shall come to pass, when I bring a cloud over the earth, that the bow shall be seen in the cloud: And I will remember My covenant, which is between Me and you and every living creature of all flesh; and the waters shall no more become a flood to destroy all flesh" (Genesis 9:8,

13-15). The rainbow is a demonstration of God's sovereignty in nature.

God in His providential kindness "maketh His sun to rise on the evil and on the good, and sendeth rain on the just and on the unjust" (Matthew 5:45). Here is a fixed law in nature well known to all. Yet such is His dominion over nature that, in judgment upon an apostate people, He declared, "I have withholden the rain from you, when there were yet three months to the harvest: and I caused it to rain upon one city, and caused it not to rain upon another city: one piece was rained upon, and the piece whereupon it rained not withered. So two or three cities wandered unto one city, to drink water; but they were not satisfied: yet have ye not returned unto Me" (Amos 4:7-8). Surely as the Psalmist wrote: "He causeth the vapours to ascend from the ends of the earth; He maketh lightnings for the rain; He bringeth the wind out of His treasuries" (Psalm 135:7).

God also rules over humanity in spite of the obdurate and rebellious will of mankind. Nebuchadnezzar, king of Babylon, made some very bold and emphatic declarations after he had been taught some very bitter lessons. He himself describes these lessons: "There fell a voice from heaven, saying, O king Nebuchadnezzar, to thee it is spoken; The kingdom is departed from thee. And they shall drive thee from men, and thy dwelling shall be with the beasts of the field: they shall make thee to eat grass as oxen, and seven times shall pass over thee, until thou know that the most High ruleth in the kingdom of men, and giveth it to whomsoever He will" (Daniel 4:31-32).

On his recovery Nebuchadnezzar made this royal declaration: "And at the end of the days I Nebuchadnezzar lifted up mine eyes unto heaven, and mine understanding returned unto me, and I blessed the most High, and I praised and honoured Him that liveth for ever, whose dominion is an everlasting dominion, and His kingdom is from generation to generation: And all the inhabitants of the earth are reputed as nothing: and He doeth according to His will in the army of heaven, and among the inhabitants of the earth: and none can stay His hand, or say unto Him, What doest Thou?'' (Daniel 4:34-35)

It is very interesting that Sir H. Rawlinson quotes Nebuchadnezzar himself as relating his inactivity of some years. This may be a hint of the period of his insanity.[1]

One of the Jehovic titles that indicates God's rule over all celestial beings is ''the Lord of Hosts,'' for the armies of Heaven all do His bidding. ''Our God is in the heavens: He hath done whatsoever He hath pleased'' (Psalm 115:3). Another psalmist asserts, ''Whatsoever the LORD pleased, that He did in heaven, and in earth, in the seas, and all deep places'' (Psalm 135:6). Moses records in the Pentateuch, ''Jacob went on his way, and the angels of God met him. And when Jacob saw them, he said, This is God's host: and he called the name of that place Mahanaim'' (Genesis 32:1-2). Their presence must have strengthened him for he was now ready to go forth and meet his brother even though Esau did have an army of four hundred armed men.

History reveals that God intimated His willingness to be a theocratic monarch over the nation He had raised up from the family of Abraham. Moses, in his recapitulation of the way by which God had led His people throughout their years in the wilderness, says, ''And He was king of Jeshurun'' (Deuteronomy 33:5). Jeshurun was an honorable name given to Israel and represented her as a good and honorable nation. Alas, Moses also had to record, ''Jeshurun waxed fat, and kicked . . . then forsook God which made him, and lightly esteemed the Rock of his salvation'' (Deuteronomy 32:15).

Poor Balaam, on looking down upon Israel's mountains of

---

[1]Jamieson, Fausset, and Brown, *Commentary, Old Testament,* page 629.

Moab without discerning the attitude of departure from God in the hearts of the nation, said, "The LORD his God is with him, and the shout of a king is among them. God brought them out of Egypt; He hath as it were the strength of an unicorn" (Numbers 23:21-22). The next day as Balaam again viewed Israel from the hilltops and uttered the inspired blessing, he said, "His king shall be higher than Agag, and his kingdom shall be exalted" (Numbers 24:7). Agag was the name given to all the kings of the Amalekites, and they were the most powerful people known to Israel. Balaam was implying that Israel's king would be higher than the highest. This indeed will ultimately be true.

This cursory survey of the insignia of theocracy in Israel only deepens the grief of heart produced by God's words to Samuel, "Hearken unto the voice of the people in all that they say unto thee; for they have not rejected thee, but they have rejected Me, that I should not reign over them" (1 Samuel 8:7).

History also testifies that although rejected by Israel, God in Christ presented Himself again as King to the nation and was once more rejected. Their attitude was, "We will not have this man to reign over us" (Luke 19:14). They consequently told Pilate, "We have no king but Caesar" (John 19:15). Since then they have suffered under the power of many Gentile Caesars.

In Mystery

A study of divine sovereignty in apostolic and contemporary times requires some understanding of the three terms: mystery, the kingdom of Heaven, and the kingdom of God.

Mystery. Unfortunately we usually have attached only one of several meanings to this English word. What is considered a mystery is thought to be inexplicable. This word is not used exclusively in this sense in Holy Scripture. In the New Testament it denotes that which cannot be apprehended by natural means, but only by divine revelation. Furthermore, it also denotes that which is secret with God. Mysteries were revealed directly by the Lord to such as the Apostle Paul, and likewise to those whom He enlightened by His Spirit. Revelations were given by God at the times He Himself had appointed.

Dr. Merrill Unger in his *Bible Dictionary* gives an excellent statement:

> The New Testament use of the term "mystery" has reference to some operation or plan of God hitherto unrevealed. It does not carry the idea of a secret to be withheld, but to be published (1 Corinthians 4:1). Paul uses the word twenty-one times. The term mystery, moreover, comprehends not only a previously hidden truth, presently divulged, but one that contains a supernatural element which still remains in spite of the revelation.[1]

Dr. Unger then lists eleven mysteries in the New Testament.

Certain societies among men have their mysteries, secrets which are made known only to the initiated. Using this as an illustration, we may assume that the disciples were initiates. The Lord said to them, "It is given unto you to know the mysteries of the kingdom of heaven, but to them [the multitude that had gathered] it is not given" (Matthew 13:11).

The kingdom of Heaven. It has been repeatedly stated that while the Church is not the kingdom, the Church is in the kingdom. This dictum is true only if we limit the word Church to the contemporary Church, that part of it that is still on earth. The children of the kingdom of God are in the Church, but the kingdom of God must not be constricted to the concept of the Church. When a baby is born in Ontario, it is likewise born into Canada. Similarly, when a child is

---

[1]*Unger's Bible Dictionary*, page 769.

born in New Jersey, it also is born into the United States of America. The smaller area is contained in the larger.

As we by experience learn to distinguish between provincial or state and federal affairs, as these touch our lives, even so we must learn to make distinctions among Biblical matters, in order that we may know how these are to influence our lives.

There are some who affirm that the kingdom of God and the kingdom of Heaven are identically the same in meaning, they are synonymous terms. They base this conclusion on the fact that on a few occasions these terms are used interchangeably. In this regard it should be noticed that the term "kingdom of heaven" is used only by Matthew; whereas "the kingdom of God" is used by all four of the Evangelists: Matthew, Mark, Luke, and John.

The kingdom of heaven, or as it should be rendered, the kingdom of the heavens, has to do with even a professed submission to God's rule over men at any period of time. The concept of the kingdom of God is much more comprehensive; it apparently includes all, in both Heaven and on earth, who are God's voluntary subjects and who consequently love and commune with Him.

The kingdom of the heavens is limited to time, but the kingdom of God is eternal. One may be born physically into the kingdom of the heavens, or even enter it by living an honorable life, professing to know the Lord. The Lord said to the multitude that ascended the mountain to hear Him, "I say unto you, That except your righteousness shall exceed the righteousness of the scribes and Pharisees, ye shall in no case enter into the kingdom of heaven" (Matthew 5:20). In contrast, one must be born by the Spirit of God to enter the kingdom of God. The Lord Jesus told Nicodemus, "Except a man be born of water and of the Spirit, he cannot enter into the kingdom of God" (John 3:5).

One through birth or righteous living may find himself

within the kingdom of Heaven, and yet unfortunately never through the new birth have entered into the kingdom of God.

The present form of the kingdom. It frequently has been said that during the present age the kingdom is in mystery form; or, as others say, in spiritual form. As has been noticed, the word mystery in this connection means a divine secret, a divine secret with hidden depths. The understanding of these divine secrets of the kingdom of Heaven was given exclusively to Christ's disciples. Concerning the multitude the Lord said, "Therefore speak I to them in parables: because they seeing see not; and hearing they hear not, neither do they understand" (Matthew 13:13).

Matthew has preserved for us the seven parables spoken by our Lord at that time. These reveal the moral character of the kingdom of Heaven from apostolic days to the end of this present age. In the first parable the Word of God as precious seed is sown in the hearts of His hearers, but only a very limited amount germinates, develops, and brings forth fruit; the majority remains lifeless, unproductive in unbelief. In the second, tares are sown by an enemy in a field of wheat. These are permitted to grow together until harvest when the tares will be gathered and destroyed but the wheat will be preserved.

The third parable pictures a monstrosity: what should have been only a shrub becomes a huge tree; rooted in the earth it filled the entire world. What a picture of professing Christendom—Christendom with all its flying and roosting perversions. The fourth parable stretches this picture even further. Here the democracy, compromise, and defection of Christendom continues as in a process of fermentation.

The fifth and sixth parables present the Lord giving up His riches to become poor in order to purchase both the treasure in the field and the pearl of great price. The first of these, the treasure in the field, is out of the land, redeemed Israel. The second is out of the sea, out from among the nations, the Church. Souls redeemed from among all nations form the Church, the body of Christ.

The seventh parable leads us in thought to the end of this age, to the end of the "times of the Gentiles," those days just previous to the revelation of the Son of man. Then the redeemed will be separated from the impenitent; the wicked will be destroyed and the righteous left to enter with Christ into His millennial kingdom.

Students of prophecy consider Nebuchadnezzar's ascendancy over Judah and the captivity of the latter in Babylon as the beginning of the period referred to by our Lord as the "times [years] of the Gentiles." This time, which has been one of suffering for the Jewish people and will continue to be so unto the end, will close with the triumph of the Lord Jesus as King of kings and Lord of lords. The Apostle John describes this prophetic scene as if it were history: "And I saw the beast, and the kings of the earth, and their armies, gathered together to make war against Him that sat on the horse, and against His army. And the beast was taken, and with him the false prophet that wrought miracles before him, with which he deceived them that had received the mark of the beast, and them that worshipped his image. These both were cast alive into a lake of fire burning with brimstone" (Revelation 19:19-20).

It is interesting to notice that the last three of these parables were spoken by the Lord in the house where He was alone with His disciples.

Each one of these parables represents a strange mixture of the genuine and the spurious, with the spurious being predominant. This then is the divine delineation of the kingdom of Heaven, part of which is known as Christendom.

The kingdom of God. As the kingdom of Heaven brings

profession clearly into view, even so the kingdom of God discloses the genuine, the real, and the true. Let its spiritual aspect first be considered for although the kingdom of God is not yet manifested, it nevertheless exists.

1. *Entrance into the kingdom of God.* This is by a spiritual birth. The Lord Jesus said to the Jewish rabbi, Nicodemus, "Except a man be born of water and of the Spirit, he cannot enter into the kingdom of God" (John 3:5). This is equivalent to being "delivered from the power of darkness, and being translated into the kingdom of His dear Son" (Colossians 1:13).

There is no implication that water here is a symbol of baptism. C. F. Hogg, in his volume on answering scriptural difficulties, states that inasmuch as the preposition "that" may also be translated "even," this text may correctly read, "Except a man be born of water even the Spirit, he cannot enter into the kingdom of God."[1]

The act of baptism may be indicative of obedience on the part of a believer, but it does not in anywise contribute to his salvation.

2. *Calling into the kingdom of God.* This indeed is a calling on high (Philippians 3:14). The young believers at Thessalonica were exhorted that they should walk worthy of God, who had called them into His kingdom and glory (1 Thessalonians 2:12).

There are some texts in this passage which intimate that the Lord is constantly calling us as if He were wooing us away from all else to be exclusively for Himself. He calls us into His kingdom which at the present is in mystery form, because the King of the kingdom Himself is absent from earth. Eventually when Christ the Supreme Sovereign returns, the kingdom will be fully manifested. All believers shall then share His

---

[1]C. F. Hogg, *What Saith the Scripture?* London, Pickering and Inglis, page 145.

glory, the glory to which He has called them. Undoubtedly the kingdom and the King were major themes in Paul's preaching at Thessalonica.

The charge that the enemies of the gospel laid against Paul and his colleagues was, "These all do contrary to the decree of Caesar, saying that there is another king, one Jesus" (Acts 17:7).

King of my life,
I crown Thee now,
Thine shall the glory be;
Lest I forget
Thy thorn-crowned brow,
Lead me to Calvary.

JENNIE EVELYN HUSSEY

3. *Proper conduct within the kingdom of God.* Christ's sermon on the Mount (Matthew 5—7) presents the principles of righteousness and fidelity which are meant to have perpetual and comprehensive application. While it is true that they will govern the kingdom of God in its manifestation, it is equally true that they are binding upon all subjects of the kingdom now, even though the King is absent.

The Sermon on the Mount opens with the beatitudes. In these remarkable sayings, the King, the Supreme Sovereign, gives a portrait of Himself.

"Blessed are the poor in spirit." "Ye know the grace of our Lord Jesus Christ, that, though He was rich, yet for your sakes He became poor [in spiritual and in material things], that ye, through His poverty might be rich" (2 Corinthians 8:9).

"Blessed are they that mourn." "A man of sorrows, and acquainted with grief" (Isaiah 53:3).

"Blessed are the meek." "I am meek and lowly in heart" (Matthew 11:29).

"Blessed are they which do hunger and thirst after

righteousness." "I do always those things that please [the Father]" (John 8:29).

"Blessed are the merciful." "He was moved with compassion on them" (Matthew 9:36).

"Blessed are the pure in heart." "Holy, harmless, undefiled, separate from sinners" (Hebrews 7:26).

"Blessed are the peace makers." "Being justified by faith, we have peace with God through our Lord Jesus Christ" (Romans 5:1).

These principles of righteousness and fidelity should deeply influence each subject in the kingdom of God, particularly during the absence of the King Himself. This brief and partial survey of the beatitudes suggests that the more the believer applies these principles in practice in his life, the more will he become like Christ. "We all, with open face beholding as in a glass the glory of the Lord, are changed into the same image from glory to glory, even as by the Spirit of the Lord" (2 Corinthians 3:18).

4. *Compensations in the kingdom of God.* After the rapture of the Church, believers will appear before the judgment seat of Christ, not in fear of being penalized; the Word of God assures them of this: "There is therefore now no condemnation to them which are in Christ Jesus" (Romans 8:1). They will be there in order that their lives will be reviewed, and that they will receive a reward or suffer a loss. "For we must all appear before the judgment seat of Christ; that every one may receive the things done in his body, according to that he hath done, whether it be good or bad" (2 Corinthians 5:10).

The rewards which may then be received have been discussed in an earlier chapter; they are called crowns: the crown of life for the martyr (Revelation 2:10), the crown of glory for the pastor (1 Peter 5:4), the crown of rejoicing for the evangelist (1 Thessalonians 2:19), the incorruptible crown for the victor (1 Corinthians 9:25), the crown of righteousness for those who long for the return of the Lord Jesus (Titus 2:13; 2 Timothy 4:8).

According to some of the kingdom parables spoken by the Lord, these crowns represent positions of authority in the administration of the Messianic kingdom of the future. Some saints will be placed over ten cities, some over five, some over only one; rewards won now through love, loyalty, and fidelity will then be fully manifest.

They will become tokens of worship. In vision John saw "The four and twenty elders [representing the Church in priestly capacity] fall down before Him that sat on the throne, and worship Him that liveth for ever and ever, and cast their crowns before the throne, saying, Thou art worthy, O Lord, to receive glory and honour and power: for Thou hast created all things, and for Thy pleasure they are and were created" (Revelation 4:10-11).

In Prophecy

Certain prophecies, especially those related to the coming of Christ, have a double reference; they are telescopic in character; that is, they can distinguish events at two different distances. The element of time seems to be ignored in such predictive passages. For example, Isaiah asserts, "Unto us a child is born, unto us a son is given: and the government shall be upon His shoulder: and His name shall be called Wonderful, Counsellor, The mighty God, The everlasting Father, The Prince of Peace. Of the increase of His government and peace there shall be no end, upon the throne of David, and upon his kingdom, to order it, and to establish it with judgment and with justice from henceforth even for ever" (Isaiah 9:6-7). The prophet predicts both advents of Christ without any mention of the prolonged period between.

Christ's first advent is prophesied in the statement, "Unto

us a child is born, unto us a son is given," whereas His second advent to earth is revealed in the remainder of the text, "And the government shall be upon His shoulder," etc.

A similar double reference appears as Micah foretells the coming of Israel's Messiah: "Thou, Bethlehem Ephratah, though thou be little among the thousands of Judah, yet out of thee shall He come forth unto Me that is to be ruler in Israel; whose goings forth have been of old, from everlasting" (Micah 5:2).

The Spirit of God sums up the importance of this double reference in prophecy in the words of the Apostle Peter: "Of which salvation the prophets have enquired and searched diligently, who prophesied of the grace that should come unto you: searching what, or what manner of time the Spirit of Christ which was in them did signify, when it testified beforehand the sufferings of Christ, and the glory that should follow" (1 Peter 1:10-11).

When the prophecies in Isaiah and Micah were written all the details were then future, yet the two major elements in each were many centuries apart. It is difficult for us to imagine how frustrating all this must have been to those holy men. Eventually "it was revealed, that not unto themselves, but unto us they did minister the things, which are now reported to you by them that have preached the gospel unto you with the Holy Spirit sent down from heaven" (1 Peter 1:12).

The Return of the Sovereign

In such double reference passages as well as in many others the Supreme Sovereign is described. He is portrayed as being born of a virgin mother, Mary of Nazareth (Luke 1:26-35; 2:1-7), and as a descendant of Abraham to whom specific promises regarding Him were made: "To Abraham and his seed were the promises made. He saith not, And to seeds, as of many; but as of one, and to thy seed, which is Christ" (Galatians 3:16).

Although Christ performed an expansive priestly work in putting away sin by the sacrifice of Himself, He was not of the tribe of Levi. The Biblical description assures us "that our Lord sprang out of Judah; of which tribe Moses spake nothing concerning priesthood" (Hebrews 7:14). He likewise is pictured as being "made of the seed of David according to the flesh; And declared to be the Son of God with power" (Romans 1:3-4).

Racially this glorious King is of the seed of Abraham; nationally, of the seed of David; humanly, of the seed of the woman; and eternally, the Son of God.

"God sent forth His Son, made of a woman" (Galatians 4:4) to atone for human sin; to defeat the strong one, Satan; ultimately to assume the responsibility of world dominion and to manifest Himself in infinite glory and majesty.

The return of Christ the King will be in vivid contrast to His first advent to earth. When He came as God incarnate to Bethlehem, He came in gracious humility. He Himself said at that time, "Learn of Me; for I am meek and lowly in heart: and ye shall find rest unto your souls" (Matthew 11:29).

The Lord Jesus predicted the manner of His second coming, His coming to establish His kingdom: "For as the lightning cometh out of the east, and shineth even unto the west; so shall the coming of the Son of Man be. . . . And then shall appear the sign of the Son of man in heaven: and then shall all the tribes of the earth mourn, and they shall see the Son of man coming in the clouds of heaven with power and great glory. . . . Watch therefore: for ye know not what hour your Lord doth come. . . . Therefore be ye also ready; for in such an hour as ye think not the Son of man cometh" (Matthew 24:27,30,42,44).

The New Testament establishes beyond all doubt that the

first stage of Christ's return will result in the rapture of the Church to Heaven. All believers of this era will be caught up to meet the Lord in the air. Inasmuch as this subject has already been discussed, attention here will be focused upon Christ's coming to fulfill His promises to His chosen people, Israel, and through that people to bring blessing to the entire world.

Christ's coming to earth as King *will be sudden and visible.* "Every eye shall see Him, and they also which pierced Him: and all kindreds of the earth shall wail because of Him" (Revelation 1:7).

The coming of the King *will also be victorious.* His triumphant return is pictured by Daniel in his interpretation of the dream of Nebuchadnezzar. "And in the days of these kings shall the God of heaven set up a kingdom, which shall never be destroyed: and the kingdom shall not be left to other people, but it shall break in pieces and consume all these kingdoms, and it shall stand for ever. Forasmuch as thou sawest that the stone was cut out of the mountain without hands, and that it break in pieces the iron, the brass, the clay, the silver, and the gold; the great God hath made known to the king what shall come to pass hereafter" (Daniel 2:44-45).

John in his vision on Patmos sees it all as if it had already happened: "Out of His mouth goeth a sharp sword, that with it He should smite the nations: and He shall rule them with a rod of iron: and He treadeth the winepress of the fierceness and wrath of Almighty God. And He hath on His vesture . . . a name written, KING OF KINGS, AND LORD OF LORDS" (Revelation 19:15-16).

The King's return *will in many respects be catastrophic.* "For thus saith the LORD of hosts; Yet once, it is a little while, and I will shake the heavens, and the earth, and the sea, and the dry land; and I will shake all nations" (Haggai 2:6-7).

Samuel intimated that Saul was the desire of all Israel (1 Samuel 9:20). Similarly Israel's Messiah is spoken of in Haggai as "the desire of all nations." Elsewhere He is spoken of as "the desire of woman." Jewish mothers from generation to generation have hoped that their male child would be the desired one, the Messiah. The future king of the Jews, an apostate usurper, will have no regard for the God of His fathers, nor for "the desire of woman" (Daniel 11:37). In spite of such opposition Haggai prophesied, "The desire of all nations shall come: and I will fill this house with glory, saith the LORD of hosts" (Haggai 2:7).

Here is another double reference passage. There is no doubt but that the Lord would honor the remnant of Israel as they sought to rebuild the temple that had been destroyed, but Israel's millennial temple is also in view. The sanctuary to be built in the very center of the nation's oblation to the Lord (Ezekiel 48:21) will be filled with glory.

In the Epistle to the Hebrews the Spirit of God gives an explanation of the worldwide upheavals: "This word, Yet once more, signifieth the removing of those things that are shaken, as of things that are made, that those things which cannot be shaken may remain" (Hebrews 12:27).

Christ will return as *the Son of man in a judicial role.* "When the Son of man shall come in His glory. . . . And before Him shall be gathered all nations: and He shall separate them one from another, as a shepherd divideth his sheep from the goats: And He shall set the sheep on His right hand, but the goats on the left. Then shall the King say unto them on His right hand, Come, ye blessed of My Father, inherit the kingdom prepared for you from the foundation of the world" (Matthew 25:31-34). Christ will come as the Supreme Sovereign to deal with all sin and rebellion and to inaugurate a reign of peace, righteousness, and justice.

"Gird Thy sword upon Thy thigh, O most mighty, with Thy glory and Thy majesty. . . . Who is this King of glory?

The LORD strong and mighty, the LORD mighty in battle. Lift up your heads, O ye gates; even lift them up, ye everlasting doors; and the King of glory shall come in. Who is this King of glory? The LORD of hosts, He is the King of glory. Selah. . . . Yet have I set My king upon My holy hill of Zion'' (Psalm 45:3; 24:8-10; 2:6).

All hail the power of Jesus' name!
    Let angels prostrate fall;
Bring forth the royal diadem,
    And crown Him Lord of all!
Let every kindred, every tribe,
    On this terrestrial ball,
To Him all majesty ascribe,
    And crown Him Lord of all!
O that with yonder sacred throng
    We at His feet may fall!
We'll join the everlasting song,
    And crown Him Lord of all!

EDWARD PERRONET

12

THE THEOCRATIC DOMINION

''The LORD hath prepared His throne in the heavens; and His kingdom ruleth over all'' (Psalm 103:19). ''The LORD sitteth King for ever'' (Psalm 29:10).

The Biblical idea of sovereignty is not that of the constitutional monarch of today; it, rather, is that of one possessing both authority and power, the authority to rule and the power to enforce that authority. Thoughts of the majesty, authority, and power of God should lead us to exclaim with David, ''I will extol Thee, my God, O King; and I will bless Thy name for ever and ever'' (Psalm 145:1).

There are two anonymous psalms which open with the assertion, ''The Lord reigneth.'' Both of these illustrate the imposition of authority by power. The first reads, ''The LORD reigneth; let the earth rejoice; let the multitude of isles be glad'' (Psalm 97:1). The second one reads, ''The LORD reigneth; let the people tremble: He sitteth between the cherubims; let the earth be moved'' (Psalm 99:1). God's sovereignty can produce joy, peace, and rest; or trembling, terror, and consternation.

When the Lord Jesus, the Son of David and the Son of man, eventually returns to earth as the King of kings and the Lord of lords, He will rule both nationally and universally.

The benign reign of the exalted Christ begins with the imprisonment for one thousand years of the archenemy of God and man. ''I saw,'' says John, ''an angel come down from heaven, having the key of the bottomless pit and a great chain in his hand. And he laid hold on the dragon, that old serpent, which is the Devil, and Satan, and bound him a thousand years, and cast him into the bottomless pit, and shut him up, that he should deceive the nations no more, till the thousand years be fulfilled'' (Revelation 20:1-3).

The Lord Jesus clothed Himself in humanity ''that . . . He might destroy him that had the power of death, that is, the devil'' (Hebrews 2:14). Furthermore, ''For this purpose the Son of God was manifested, that He might destroy the works of the devil'' (1 John 3:8). Satan's power has been broken, but as he awaits his execution and his final end, he is still ''the great dragon . . . that old serpent, called the Devil, and Satan, which deceiveth the whole world'' (Revelation 12:9).

During the millennium man will live under the most benevolent conditions possible. If a new environment would effect a change, in these remarkable circumstances that change would promptly appear, and would the more progressively manifest itself.

The national kingdom. Numerous details are given in Scripture of the reign of our Lord over a restored, united, and richly blessed Israel.

1. It was predicted of Christ, before He was born of Mary, that as the Son of the Highest ''He shall be great . . . and the Lord God shall give unto Him the throne of His father David: and He shall reign over the house of Jacob for ever; and of His kingdom there shall be no end'' (Luke 1:32-33).

The Lord Jesus is assured of that regal position through God's covenant with David: ''The word of the LORD came unto Jeremiah, saying, Thus saith the LORD; If ye can break My covenant of the day, and My covenant of the night, and that there should not be day and night in their season; then may also My covenant be broken with David My servant, that he should not have a son to reign upon his throne; and with the Levites the priests, My ministers'' (Jeremiah 33:19-20).

"Behold the Man" (Zechariah 6:12). The Man par excellence—the Ideal and Representative of the race, who, after having for our salvation worn the crown of thorns, shall, as the reward of His sufferings, be "crowned with glory and honour," and have all things put under His feet.

"Behold the Man!" "Behold My Servant!" (Isaiah 42:1; 52:13), "Behold thy King!" (Zechariah 9:9), "Behold your God!" (Isaiah 40:9); thus variously, as calling attention to the different aspects of the character of the same blessed Person, is this word "Behold" used by God Himself.[1]

2. Jerusalem in that day will not only be the capital city of the nation of Israel, but it will be the metropolis of the whole earth. Then the words of the Psalmist will be true: "Beautiful for situation, the joy of the whole earth, in mount Zion, on the sides of the north, the city of the great King" (Psalm 48:2). The author in his poetry indicates how very distinguished Jerusalem will then be. "On the sides of the north" was figurative language among the ancients used to impress others. Here it is meant to show the eminence of that beautiful capital city. Satan as Lucifer, in his pride and arrogance, used the very same expression to indicate the prominence and exaltation to which he aspired (Isaiah 14:12-14).

In that day apparently there will be access to the great city by water and land, and probably by air: "And His feet [the feet of the Messiah] shall stand in that day upon the mount of Olives, which is before Jerusalem on the east, and the mount of Olives shall cleave in the midst thereof toward the east and toward the west, and there shall be a very great valley; and half of the mountain shall remove toward the north, and half of it toward the south. . . . And it shall be in that day, that living waters shall go out from Jerusalem; half of them toward the former sea, and half of them toward the hinder sea: in

---

[1]David Baron, *The Visions and Prophecies of Zechariah,* London: Hebrew Christian Testimony to Israel, page 191.

summer and in winter shall it be. And the LORD shall be king over all the earth: in that day there shall be one LORD, and His name one" (Zechariah 14:4-11).

According to the news media, the Israeli government plans to make just such a waterway from the Mediterranean Sea down to the Dead Sea. One of the major purposes of such a task when it is finished is to generate electricity by hydro power. Certain geologists have published their conclusion that there is a definite rift along this route, and stretching even into Africa. Such is the magnitude of this fissure that it could open up with not too severe an earthquake.

3. Not only will Israel have her King and a great capital city, but she will again have a temple. One of the first acts of the King when He begins His reign will be to erect a magnificent temple. This temple of the millennium must not be confused with the temple in which the antichrist will enshrine himself. "Behold, the man whose name is The BRANCH; and He shall grow up out of His place, and He shall build the temple of the LORD: even He shall build the temple of the LORD; and He shall bear the glory, and shall sit and rule upon His throne; and He shall be a priest upon His throne: and the counsel of peace shall be between them both" (Zechariah 6:12-13).

When Israel in the days of Ezra rebuilt the Temple destroyed by Nebuchadnezzar, Joshua and Zerubbabel worked together, Joshua representing the priesthood and Zerubbabel the civil authorities. In that future time of glory and righteousness "peace shall be perfectly ensured by the concurrence of the two offices in the one Messiah, who by His mediatorial priesthood purchased it, and by His kingly rule maintains it."[1]

Ezekiel informs us that in those days of peace and tranquility the restored nation will return to the Lord a large obla-

[1]Jamieson, Fausset, and Brown, *Commentary, Old Testament,* page 724.

tion of land 25,000 reeds square. A reed is approximately eleven feet in linear measure. Seven tribes will receive their allotment of land to the west of this oblation, and the remaining five will receive theirs to the east.

This large oblation will be divided into three parts. The first part, 10,000 by 25,000 reeds, apparently will be for the Levites. The second part, of the same dimensions, is for the priests. Concerning this section we read: "And for them, even for the priests, shall be this holy oblation; toward the north five and twenty thousand in length, and toward the west ten thousand in breadth, and toward the east ten thousand in breadth, and toward the south five and twenty thousand in length: and the sanctuary of the LORD shall be in the midst thereof" (Ezekiel 48:10). Consequently we conclude that the millennial temple will be in the very center of the oblation.

The remaining section of the oblation is smaller than the others. It is 5,000 by 25,000 reeds, and therein lies the city of Jerusalem.

It has been said that the builders of Herod's temple, which was destroyed by the Roman soldiers under Titus in A.D. 70, were greatly influenced in their plans by reading about the temple in the book of Ezekiel.

4. The true Church in the celebration of the Lord's Supper commemorates the sorrow, suffering, and death of the Lord Jesus and His accomplishments on the cross at Calvary. During the millennium the offerings of sacrifices will be resumed; these will all be commemorative.

Old Testament sacrifices and offerings were all in anticipation of the coming of the Saviour. Thank God He came and in Him all the types and shadows were fulfilled. The sacrifices during the millennium will be in retrospect.

The Aaronic priesthood failed and this failure is seen in the death of Eli and his two wicked sons. In the battle with the Philistines at Ebenezer, "the ark of God was taken; and the two sons of Eli, Hophni and Phinehas, were slain. . . . And it came to pass, when he [the messenger] made mention of the ark of God, that he [Eli] fell from off the seat backward by the side of the gate, and his neck brake, and he died'' (1 Samuel 4:11,18).

After the tragedy, God raised up Samuel, a real man of God, to direct Israel through that grave crisis.

With the development and the uniting of the nation under David, and its ascendancy in power and glory, ''Zadok the son of Ahitub, and Ahimelech the son of Abiathar, were the priests'' (2 Samuel 8:17). Later, after the death of David, ''Zadok the priest did the king [Solomon] put in the room of Abiathar'' (1 Kings 2:35). Zadok then was the high priest when the nation reached its zenith of power, influence, and glory. During Messiah's reign of peace, righteousness, and splendor, ''the priests the Levites, the sons of Zadok, that kept the charge of My sanctuary when the children of Israel went astray from Me, they shall come near to Me to minister unto Me, and they shall stand before Me to offer unto Me the fat and the blood, saith the Lord GOD'' (Ezekiel 44:15).

In those days of resplendent glory Israel will become the head and not the tail of the nations. ''And many people shall go and say, Come ye, and let us go up to the mountain of the LORD, to the house of the God of Jacob; and He will teach us of His ways, and we will walk in His paths: for out of Zion shall go forth the law, and the Word of the LORD from Jerusalem'' (Isaiah 2:3).

Universal theocratic dominion. The Lord has ever been the universal Sovereign. Irrespective of human behavior expressing rebellion, denial, and rejection, God has always ruled among the kingdoms of men. As Nebuchadnezzar was forced to admit: ''[His] dominion is an everlasting dominion, and His kingdom is from generation to generation: And all the inhabitants of the earth are reputed as nothing . . . none can stay His hand, or say unto Him, What doest Thou?" (Daniel 4:34-35)

When our Lord Jesus returns to earth with His then perfect consort, there will be many recoveries to states known formerly in a noncursed earth. There will be very many changes and transformations.

"The bondage of corruption" expresses very concisely and forcefully the condition of the earth as cursed for man's sake. The slow processes of decay; the catastrophic destruction of land and property caused by disruptions of nature; the blight that frequently befalls the vegetable kingdom; the devastation caused by insects, grubs, and other pests; these are all included in the one word corruption. So inexorable is this condition that, in spite of man's scientific efforts to arrest the progress of the ruinous consequences, there is no liberation from the bondgage. Nor can there be any until the Creator Himself intervenes. Then "the creation itself also shall be delivered from the bondage of corruption into the glorious liberty of the children of God. For we know that the whole creation groaneth and travaileth in pain together until now. And not only they, but ourselves also, which have the firstfruits of the Spirit, even we ourselves groan within ourselves, waiting for the adoption, to wit, the redemption of our body" (Romans 8:21-23).

If for man's sake alone the earth was cursed, it cannot surprise us that it should share in his recovery. And if so, to represent it as sympathizing with man's miseries, and a looking forward to his complete redemption in the period of its own emancipation from its present sin-blighted condition, is a beautiful thought, and in harmony with the general teaching of Scripture.[1]

1. The earth will appear as a botanical garden. How beautiful Eden must have been! A sinless world, an uncursed

---

[1]Jamieson, Fausset, and Brown, *Commentary, New Testament,* page 241.

earth are far beyond human imagination. To enjoy the perfect beauty of flourishing uninfected plants, to inhale the pleasant aroma of the garden of Eden, and to sense the specific fragrance from nature's distilleries of the most exquisite perfumes are all beyond man's complete idealism.

The phrase a "garden in Eden, in the east" makes it clear that Eden is a locality here, not a symbol. Genesis 2:8-14 goes to some length to present it as an actual, not an allegorical or mythical spot.[1]

Because of sin nature now hides much of her extravagant loveliness; nevertheless the flora and the fauna of each particular region are fascinating. The exotic flowers of the flat barrens of the north and the profuse blooms of the tropical and semitropical areas delight the aesthetic nature of man.

There is also a beauty that man never sees. The cactus that flourishes in the depth of the desert shows its loveliness alone to its Creator. Well might David say in one of his poems, "The earth is the LORD's and the fulness thereof" (Psalm 24:1).

Notwithstanding the form and the comeliness of this world in which man lives, he lives on a cursed earth: "Because thou hast . . . eaten of the tree, of which I commanded thee, saying, Thou shalt not eat of it: cursed is the ground for thy sake; in sorrow shalt thou eat of it all the days of thy life; Thorns also and thistles shall it bring forth to thee; and thou shalt eat the herb of the field" (Genesis 3:17-18).

Thorns . . . and thistles are the eloquent signs of nature's untamed and encroaching; in the Old Testament they mark the scene of man's self-defeat and God's judgment, e.g., the sluggard's field (Proverbs 24:31) and the ruined city (Isaiah 34:13). They need not be envisaged as newly created, but as henceforth a perennial threat; for man in his own disorder would never now subdue the earth.

---

[1]Derek Kidner, "Genesis" in *Tyndale Commentaries,* page 62.

The nature miracles of Jesus give some idea of the control which man under God might have exercised (cf., Hebrews 2:8-9).[1]

When the Lord Jesus, by whom all things were made (John 1:3) returns to His own creation, the earth will bloom and blossom like a botanical garden. One of the outcomes of the liberation of creation from the condition imposed because of the fall of man will be most striking and restorative: "The wilderness and the solitary place shall be glad for them; and the desert shall rejoice, and blossom as the rose. It shall blossom abundantly, and rejoice even with joy and singing: the glory of Lebanon shall be given unto it, the excellency of Carmel and Sharon, they shall see the glory of the LORD, and the excellency of our God" (Isaiah 35:1-2).

"For ye shall go out with joy, and be led forth with peace: the mountains and the hills shall break forth before you into singing, and all the trees of the field shall clap their hands. Instead of the thorn shall come up the fir tree, and instead of the brier shall come up the myrtle tree: and it shall be to the LORD for a name, for an everlasting sign that shall not be cut off" (Isaiah 55:12-13).

The long-hoped-for return of the Lord has at that time been fulfilled, and one of its blessed consequences is the restoration of the garden that was in Eden, in that kingdom of which our father Adam was monarch. The Last Adam comes, and naturally the results of the sin of the first are nullified; the chain now being closely attached, by an irrefragable link, to God, all the other inferior links are reestablished.[2]

2. If the foliage and flowers are to recover from the devastating effects of sin, is there any hope for the animal world? The fact that rapacious beasts can be tamed and snakes charmed would indicate that they were not always

---

[1]Ibid, page 62.

[2]F. C. Jennings, *Studies in Isaiah,* page 148.

what they are now, and that there was a time when man was not afraid of animals that are now ferocious, and the animals were not afraid of man.

Many species of wild life today are endangered through the covetousness and cruelty of man. If it were not that some are now protected by law more species would suffer. A book like *Death on the Ice* by Cassie Brown shows how cruel man can be both to the animals and to his fellows.

It is not difficult to classify, in a very general way, all animals. Two major groups are obvious, the vertebrates and the invertebrates. These, of course, are readily divided into smaller groups according to the environment in which they live, its latitude and its longitude. In the study of zoology their distribution must be taken into consideration: under the sea, on the earth, and in the atmosphere.

The Word of God in dealing with animal life during the millennium does not deal separately with the many varieties and with the many differences among them; it classifies them relative to their present and future state. In appearance there will be little if any change; they will still be what Adam called them. The radical change in the nature of the animals will be a contrast between what they have been for centuries and what they will be under the benign rule of the glorified Son of Jesse, the Messiah, the King.

Isaiah contrasts the carnivorous with the herbivorous animal: the wolf with the lamb; the leopard with the kid; the calf with the lion.

"The wolf also shall dwell with the lamb, and the leopard shall lie down with the kid; and the calf and the young lion and the fatling together; and a little child shall lead them. . . . They shall not hurt nor destroy in all My holy mountain: for the earth shall be full of the knowledge of the LORD, as the waters cover the sea" (Isaiah 11:6-9). "The wolf and the lamb shall feed together, and the lion shall eat straw like the bullock; and dust shall be the serpent's meat'' (Isaiah 65:25).

3. There are two major themes in the prophecy of Isaiah—judgment and redemption. While these divide the book (chapters 1—39; 30—66), concise statements covering both subjects are scattered throughout the main chapters. Notwithstanding there are astonishing statements in the closing section which deals extensively with the matter of redemption, as for example, ''The sun shall be no more thy light by day; neither for brightness shall the moon give light unto thee; but the LORD shall be unto thee an everlasting light, and thy God thy glory. The sun shall no more go down; neither shall thy moon withdraw itself: for the LORD shall be thine everlasting light, and the days of thy mourning shall be ended'' (Isaiah 60:19-20).

With the millennium the suffering, humiliation, and mourning of the Jewish people shall end. This we believe literally; therefore we must also believe literally in a great astronomical change. Are the days all over the earth to be prolonged as the days in summer above the arctic circle, where there are short periods in the year when the sun does not seem to set? For the person who believes in the inerrancy of the Word of God, such statements do not present a problem. The Creator, God Himself, who commanded, ''Let there be light: and there was light'' (Genesis 1:3-5), sustains His creation and controls its many elements and movements in order that they may fulfill His purpose.

According to the account given in Genesis 1, there was light independent of the sun. Derek Kidner in his commentary on Genesis 1 says of light, ''As it here precedes the sun, so in the final vision, it outlasts it'' (Revelation 22:5).[1]

4. A great geological change will result just prior to the

---

[1]Derek Kidner, ''Genesis,'' in *Tyndale Commentaries,* page 47.

millennium. When the Lord returns in power and glory and places His feet once more on the slopes of Olivet a rift will open, for an earthquake will follow the reappearance of the Lord Jesus on earth. God's remnant people will be terrified by their enemies and by the happenings of the day and will seek shelter: "Ye shall flee to the valley of the mountains; for the valley of the mountains shall reach unto Azal: yea, ye shall flee" (Zechariah 14:5).

As the day spoken of as Joshua's day was a prolonged day of light, so on that future occasion there will be an unusual day of gloom and semidarkness. "It shall be one day which shall be known to the LORD, not day, nor night: but it shall come to pass, that at evening time it shall be light. . . . And the LORD shall be king over all the earth: in that day shall there be one LORD, and His name one" (Zechariah 14:7-9).

5. During that glorious millennium there will be extraordinary changes in man. At the rapture of the Church, and as a result of resurrection at the close of the great tribulation, all the saints will be perfect. Those on earth will be joined by those from Heaven. John in vision saw "heaven opened, and behold a white horse; and He that sat upon him was called Faithful and True, and in righteousness He doth judge and make war. . . . And the armies which were in heaven [probably armies of both saints and angels] followed Him upon white horses, clothed in fine linen, white and clean" (Revelation 19:11-14).

In the large population that shall enter the millennium there will be a mingling together of those perfected in spiritual bodies (1 Corinthians 15:44), others who have believed in Christ as King and Saviour under the preaching of the gospel of the kingdom, during the great tribulation. These are pictured by Matthew as the sheep on His right hand (Matthew 25:33-34), but they will still be in natural bodies.

This dual state should not result in a problem. The Lord in

His resurrection body associated with His own disciples for forty days before He ascended into Heaven. He talked with them, ate with them, and dealt with their failures and shortcomings. Undoubtedly His body was different. Although in appearance the same, it no longer was confined by space, mass, or time.

> As to the mode of intercourse between the glorified and the unglorified, there are many vain speculations. We only "know in part," and time will bring the answer to our various askings. The whole discussion binds itself to our conception of the resurrection body—what it needs and what its functions are.[1]

The Lord Jesus answered certain Sadducees, "They which shall be accounted worthy to obtain that world, and the resurrection from the dead, neither marry, nor are given in marriage; Neither can they die any more; for they are equal unto the angels; and are the children of God, being the children of the resurrection" (Luke 20:35-36).

Human life will be prolonged during the millennium; Isaiah predicts: "There shall be no more thence an infant of days, nor an old man that hath not filled his days: for the child shall die an hundred years old" (Isaiah 65:20). Before the days of the Deluge man lived extremely long: Adam 930 years and Methuselah almost one thousand, actually 969 years. Sin, disease, and death have diminished man's days upon the earth. Shortly before the Deluge human life was reduced to the maximum of one hundred and twenty years. The Lord decreed, "His days shall be an hundred and twenty years" (Genesis 6:3). Moses writes of a further curtailment: "The days of our years are threescore years and ten; and if by reason of strength they be fourscore years, yet is their strength labour and sorrow; for it is soon cut off, and we fly away" (Psalm 90:10).

---

[1]Nathaniel West, *The Thousand Years,* Scripture Truth Book Company, page 319.

Furthermore, children will be born to natural parents. Isaiah again prophesied, "They shall not labour in vain, nor bring forth in trouble; for they are the seed of the blessed of the LORD, and their offspring with them" (Isaiah 65:23). "All thy children shall be taught of the LORD; and great shall be the peace of thy children" (Isaiah 54:13).

Men will then speak one language: Babel is an evidence of divine displeasure. "The LORD said, Behold, the people is one, and they have all one language; and this they begin to do [build a city and a tower in an anti-God attitude]; and now nothing will be restrained from them, which they have imagined to do. Go to, let Us go down, and there confound their language, that they may not understand one another's speech" (Genesis 11:6-7).

Pentecost with its gift of tongues breaking the language barrier was the exceeding grace of God circumventing the calamity of Babel in order that men might hear of the works of God: "They were all amazed [on that day] and marvelled, saying one to another, Behold, are not all these which speak Galileans? And how hear we every man in our own tongue, wherein we were born? . . . We do hear them speak in our tongues the wonderful works of God" (Acts 2:7-11).

After that dreadful future period of divine indignation, the great tribulation, when the Lord has crushed all His foes beneath His feet, He will return to the people a pure language. He promised, "I will turn to the people a pure language, that they may all call upon the name of the LORD, to serve Him with one consent" (Zephaniah 3:9).

A. C. Jennings in Ellicott's *Commentary* says:

> The discord of Babel shall as it were give place to unity of language, when the worship "of gods many" shall yield to the pure service of Jehovah, whom men shall with one mind and one mouth glorify.[1]

---

[1]C. J. Ellicott, *Bible Commentary*, page 542.

6. Divine administration will be perfect.

God shall demonstrate all that His goodness is capable of, and He shall reply to all of the deep aspirations which He Himself put in the heart of men. All of the excellent things which mankind has vainly sought without God shall at last be poured out in profusion in the kingdom of His dear Son.[1]

The administration of the King of kings and Lord of lords will be characterized by the stable qualities of justice, holiness, peace, and joy.

Justice. Unto the Son it was said, "Thy throne, O God, is for ever and ever: a sceptre of righteousness is the sceptre of Thy kingdom" (Hebrews 1:8).

Many are the social problems in the world today. The wrong, unequal distribution of the products of the soil has not only resulted in hungry people, but it has disturbed the minds of many conscientious persons. Injustice, so evident in man's government, wounds troubled hearts and sometimes hopelessly crushes broken lives.

During the millennial reign of our Lord, "A king shall reign in righteousness, and princes shall rule in judgment" (Isaiah 32:1). "A Branch shall grow out of his [Jesse's] roots. . . . He shall not judge after the sight of His eyes, neither reprove after the hearing of His ears: But with righteousness shall He judge the poor, and reprove with equity for the meek of the earth. . . . And righteousness shall be the girdle of His loins, and faithfulness the girdle of His reins" (Isaiah 11:1-5).

Holiness. The blessed One who sits upon the throne will rule with a rod of iron. Sin will be dealt with promptly and holiness will prevail. He shall rule the nations with a rod of iron, and dash them in pieces like a potter's vessel (Psalm 2:9).

---

[1]René Pache, *The Return of Jesus Christ,* page 399.

"In that day shall there be upon the bells of the horses, HOLINESS UNTO THE LORD: and the pots in the LORD's house shall be like the bowls before the altar. Yea, every pot in Jerusalem and in Judah shall be holiness unto the LORD" (Zechariah 14:20-21).

The character of the great Ruler will be reflected in every thing about Him. The unclean will be banished! Sin is to be crushed and the evildoer removed. The whole land is to be sanctified to God, but the city of Jerusalem is to be demonstrably set apart to Him. Even the most ordinary things of every day life are to be holy. On the mitre of Israel's high priest was a golden plate bearing the words, "Holy to Jehovah." Even the bells of the horses in that future day will bear the same inscription.

The very domestic utensils in the home are to be sanctified: everything is to be holy to God. The cauldrons used in the temple to boil the flesh of the sacrificial victims before it was eaten were now to become as holy as the sacred bowl in which the blood of the sacrifice was caught to be sprinkled upon the corners of the altar. Where the Messiah ruled, everything became sacred.[1]

Peace. With the revelation of Christ the King, the song which the shepherds heard will become true, "Glory to God in the highest, and on earth peace, and good will toward men" (Luke 2:14). This of course is to be expected, for He, the Messiah, is "the Prince of Peace" (Isaiah 9:6).

The sons of Korah prophetically sang: "Come, behold the works of the LORD, what desolations He hath made in the earth. He maketh wars to cease unto the end of the earth; He breaketh the bow, and cutteth the spear in sunder; He burneth the chariot in the fire" (Psalm 46:8-9). Then "they shall beat their swords into plowshares, and their spears into pruninghooks: nation shall not lift up sword against nation, neither shall they learn war any more" (Isaiah 2:4).

Then, and not till then, "the work of righteousness shall be peace; and the effect of righteousness quietness and

---

[1]Fredk. A. Tatford, *The Prophet of the Myrtle Grove*, page 169.

assurance for ever'' (Isaiah 32:17).

Joy. As Israel sang a song of gladness and praise immediately after their emancipation from Egypt, even so when Israel and the redeemed enter into freedom from the bondage of corruption (Romans 8:21-24) a song of salvation will arise in praise and adoration to the Lord: ''Behold, God is my salvation; I will trust, and not be afraid: for the LORD JEHOVAH is my strength and my song; He also is become my salvation. Therefore with joy shall ye draw water out of the wells of salvation'' (Isaiah 12:2-3).

''The ransomed of the LORD shall return, and come to Zion with songs and everlasting joy upon their heads: they shall obtain joy and gladness, and sorrow and sighing shall flee away'' (Isaiah 35:10).

> There is no need to write much of the beauteous scene. It is better to meditate and thus get the refreshment such lovely and well-based anticipation must give. We visit in spirit that holy mountain where alone naught defiles, where alone naught does hurt. We see the harmony of Eden renewed once more, and the wild fierce creatures of the jungle graze in the company of the fearless flocks of the farm. Still we have a hint that the scene is not one of absolute perfection, for even here we listen to an echo of that primal sentence on the serpent, for the dust shall still be his food.[1]

It has been the vain hope of many that a change of environment, an association with exemplary persons, and a new code of higher standards would elevate man and deliver him from slavery to sin. But alas we read, ''The sinner being an hundred years old shall be accursed'' (Isaiah 65:20). He will be little more than an infant, but his death will be the penalty of sin. The millennium may be a prelude to but certainly is not the eternal state, for sin and death are still very evident.

The one thousand years of righteousness, peace, and glory will end as did all other periods of human history—in failure.

---

[1]F. C. Jennings, *Studies in Isaiah*, page 749.

13

GOD ALL IN ALL

The postmillennial period described in Revelation 20 shocks one who has been enamored only by the benefits of the millennial reign of Christ. Imprisonment has not changed the ambition and the objective of Satan, nor has the one thousand years of justice and peace changed human nature. Real aggressive antagonism to God is quickly manifest under the influence of Satan, now freed from his long incarceration.

How long this postmillennial period may be is difficult to ascertain. Satan is to be loosed "a little season." The word "little" here intimates the opposite to "great." If the thousand-year period is to be considered great the little season is short only in comparison, but if the entire stretch of time is viewed as being great then "the little season" might endure for a long time. Some have suggested another thousand years. In the thinking of this author such a suggestion is not very probable.

That this additional period might actually be "the fulness of times" (Ephesians 1:10) is possible. It has been the custom among students of prophecy to apply this particular reference by the Apostle Paul to the millennium itself, but surely even then all things in Heaven and on earth are not gathered together in Christ. Perhaps we should understand this in conjunction with the prediction, "For He [Christ] must reign, till He hath put all enemies under His feet" (1 Corinthians 15:25).

Satan Loosed

"When the thousand years are expired, Satan shall be loosed out of his prison, and shall go out to deceive the nations which are in the four quarters of the earth" (Revelation 20:7).

Man's original home was a beautiful, perfect Eden, where he ruled as a monarch. When tested there by Satan's deceptive maneuvers, he fell and brought sin into the human family. After a thousand years of blessing, righteousness, and peace, man will be submitted to a final test by the same nefarious influence. Regrettably, one would say, he will readily accept the mobilization of the largest military force ever seen on earth, a mighty force to be gathered from among all the nations to do battle against God and His people. This final test will prove conclusively how incorrigible man's sinful nature is.

> He is the dragon, the personification of cruelty; the old serpent, the sinister and subtle enemy of man from the very first; the devil, the deceiver and tempter; and Satan, the constant adversary of the human race.[1]

The restraint upon Satan during the millennium being removed will provide the opportunity for a large proportion of the population to revolt. Of course, during the reign of Christ as King of kings many will be hypocritical and pretend to accept and honor Him: "The strangers shall yield feigned obedience unto Me" (Psalm 18:44, margin). The Psalmist again writes, "How terrible art Thou in Thy works! through the greatness of Thy power shall Thine enemies yield feigned obedience unto Thee" (Psalm 66:3, margin). There will be nothing feigned then. A great satanic and human confederacy will be formed to attack the capital city, the citadel of

---

[1]Fredk. A. Tatford, *Prophecy's Last Word,* page 220.

all blessing upon mankind over the whole earth during the glorious reign of the Supreme Sovereign.

The mobilization of this gigantic military force, gathered from all the points of the compass, may take considerable time. During the reign of Christ men remained untaught of tactical military schemes. Consequently there will be diplomacy among the nations in preparation for hostilities, troops will have to be trained, munitions will have to be manufactured, strategies and maneuvers will have to be developed. Of this one thing we may be assured: since they are being energized by the great adversary, Satan, matters will be expedited as quickly as possible.

The saints besieged within the Holy City will be probably God's earthly people Israel and the fruit of their testimony, the results of the preaching of the gospel of the kingdom among the millennial nations. Not all will have responded to this message; consequently many will be ready to enlist in the forces of Gog and Magog. These are not the former Gog and Magog of which Ezekiel speaks (Ezekiel 38—39) for they were completely destroyed (Ezekiel 39:1-7), but a great hostile army possessed of a similar anti-God spirit of hatred and enmity.

The complete destruction of this final rebellion is assured: "Fire came down from God out of heaven, and devoured them. And the devil that deceived them was cast into the lake of fire and brimstone, where the beast and the false prophet are, and shall be tormented day and night for ever and ever" (Revelation 20:9-10).

This rebellion of Satan and his deluded followers is not part of the millennial kingdom, but follows it. As John describes the tragic event, it does not come until "the thousand years are expired" (verse 7). Then for a brief season the divine restraint will be relaxed for the purpose of providing one last and supreme demonstration of the appalling wickedness of the unregenerated human heart.

How such a rebellion could spring up, following a kingdom which began with a society of regenerated people, should be no mystery. For regenerated parents are no guarantee of regenerated progeny, as we should have learned long ago. If the number who respond to the satanic leadership seems disappointingly large—"as the sand of the sea"—we must remember that under the millennial control of disease and death the human race will greatly multiply. Moreover, the large number of the unsaved is always balanced by the promise made to Abraham: "I will multiply thy seed as the stars of heaven, and as the sand which is upon the sea shore" (Genesis 22:17). And the saved in every age, in a sense, are Abraham's seed (Galatians 3:29). When John describes the objective of the satanic attack as "the camp of the saints" there is no necessary implication that all the millennial saints are shut up in Jerusalem. It only means that Satan recognizes, as we might expect, that here in "the beloved city" is the center or "citadel" (*parembole* of Acts 21:34) of the millennial government. The rebellion ends in judgment, not in a battle. Though Satan gathers the rebels "to battle," there is no battle. The end is the fire of divine execution.[1]

The Old Creation

From the face of the Enthroned One, "the earth and the heaven fled away" (Revelation 20:11). With this majestic rhetorical sweep the seer describes the swift and effective preparation for the final judgment of mankind. He has left others to reveal the details. The Apostle Peter asserts, "The day of the Lord will come as a thief in the night; in which the heavens shall pass away with a great noise, and the elements shall melt with fervent heat, the earth also and the works that are therein shall be burned up" (2 Peter 3:10).

Very early in human history, the Lord affirmed to Noah, "I do set My bow in the cloud. . . . And I will remember My covenant, which is between Me and you and every living

---

[1]Alva J. McClain, *The Greatness of the Kingdom,* page 508.

creature of all flesh; and the waters shall no more become a flood to destroy all flesh'' (Genesis 9:12-16). Thus with deep conviction Moses penned the assurance of the preservation of life on earth. As the rainbow is produced by both the sun and the rain, divine love and divine righteousness reveal the providential pledge that humanity would not be destroyed again by water, ''But the heavens and the earth, which are now, by the same word are kept in store, reserved unto fire against the day of judgment and perdition of ungodly men'' (2 Peter 3:7). Could the apostle's words be a Spirit-inspired reference to a future atomic destruction of the present earth and its environment?

The Final Assize

This judgment of the impenitent may be considered as the last event in the period designated the day of the Lord. There are certain who consider the appellation, the day of the Lord, as embracing only the one thousand years of the reign of our Lord as King. It appears that the Apostle Paul intimates the beginning of the day of the Lord. It will be manifest by the apostatizing from the Christian faith and the revelation of the man of sin, the Antichrist (2 Thessalonians 2:3). The Apostle Peter asserts that the day of the Lord will be characterized by the element of surprise, and that the dissolution of the present Heaven and earth will be an event within the scope of that period, but he does not claim that the flashing end of time, as we know it, represents the final close of the prolonged day of the Lord. The great white throne judgment may be the culmination of all time.

A glittering throne of great magnitude appears in space. This should present no problem for we know, as Job avers, God ''hangeth the earth upon nothing'' (Job 26:7). In many respects the earth is only a spaceship. For the Mighty Creator the elevation of a majestic court in space would present no difficulty.

The throne is white for it radiates holiness and righteousness. In this scene there is but one throne and one Judge. "Neither is there any creature that is not manifest in His sight: but all things are naked and opened unto the eyes of Him with whom we have to do" (Hebrews 4:13).

The august occupant did not always sit upon a gloriously brilliant throne; He once hung upon a cross, despised and rejected, slain. There He bore "our sins in His own body on the tree" (1 Peter 2:24). Here He will judge sin: "For as the Father hath life in Himself; so hath He given to the Son to have life in Himself; and hath given Him authority to execute judgment" (John 5:26-27). The Lord Jesus has the right to exercise His delegated powers in judgment. The Spirit of God also affirms that this He shall do, because He is the Son of man. As Son of man He was nailed to the cross for sinners (John 3:14-15). As Son of man He is the enthroned Judge.

Bullinger says:

> The title Son of man when made of Christ, with but one exception (John 5:27), has the definite article. The first man, Adam, forfeited his dominion and power through sin. No descendant of Adam shall ever have the right to universal dominion. When the Last Adam, the Son of man, comes all dominions of earth will be given Him.[1]

Prophetically Daniel declares, "There was given Him dominion, and glory, and a kingdom, that all people, nations, and languages, should serve Him: His dominion is an everlasting dominion, which shall not pass away, and His kingdom that which shall not be destroyed" (Daniel 7:14).

---

[1]E.W. Bullinger, *The Companion Bible,* appendix 98, page 144.

The Resurrection of Judgment

Jesus, in answering some of His Jewish critics, made this reference to the future resurrection: "All that are in the graves shall hear His voice, and shall come forth; they that have done good, unto the resurrection of life; and they that have done evil, unto the resurrection of damnation" (John 5:28-29). The time element between these two aspects of the resurrection was ignored by the Lord. From the context of Revelation 20 we realize that John the apostle is recording the facts regarding the latter aspect, the resurrection of judgment.

"The dead [the impenitent dead], small and great [in either stature or status, young or old] stand before God. . . . The sea gave up the dead which were in it; and death and hell delivered up the dead which were in them." The complete human personality is fully restored. Men in their former entity stand before God on this day of retribution (Revelation 20:12-13).

The books are opened; first, "the book of life." Apparently this is a complete record of the names of the redeemed. The absence of a name on this record would indicate one who is to be judged. The other books could be the history of each life, how and for whom it had been lived. "They were judged," writes John, "every man according to his works." "Whosoever was not found written in the book of life was cast into the lake of fire" (verse 15).

The last of sin and its power is cast into the lake of fire. In seeking to minimize the horror of a burning lake some contend that the language is only figurative, and this we concede it might be; but if this is only a figure, what, oh what, will the reality be?

As there is a second and higher life, so there is also a second and a deeper death. And as after that life there is no more death (21:4), so after that death there is no more life.[1]

Paul's prediction is now fulfilled, "The last enemy that shall be destroyed is death" (1 Corinthians 15:26).

The Final Triumph

"He [the Lord Jesus Christ] must reign till He hath put all enemies under His feet. The last enemy that shall be destroyed is death" (1 Corinthians 15:25-26). There can be no deviation from God's purpose; Christ must reign and conquer until full victory is assured. Death is a powerful and an aggressive opponent, but although it be the last, it will finally be abolished.

God has decreed that all things must be brought under subjection to man (Psalm 8:6). At the present, "we see not yet all things put under Him" (Hebrews 2:8).

We anticipate soon to see the complete and glorious triumph of the Son of man, the Lord from Heaven. Then shall all things be subject unto Him (1 Corinthians 15:28). Every foe eventually will be vanquished. "Then shall the Son also Himself be subject unto Him that put all things under Him."

There have been numerous abdications throughout history. Kings have been forced to renounce their thrones because of errors and impeachments, because of personal weakness and weariness, and because of national rejection, but never was there an abdication similar to this one. In the fullness of absolute and unconditional triumph the Conqueror of Golgotha subjects Himself to God. The mediatorial work that He came to do is finished. Human intellect is baffled; that One in the hour of greatest promotion and exalta-

[1]Henry Alford, *The New Testament for English Readers,* footnote, page 1931.

tion should abdicate seems incredible. Notwithstanding, it is done in order that God may be all in all.

Christ's equality with the Father and with the Divine Spirit was never at any time more manifest than now. Bible history begins with the majestic statement, "In the beginning God" (Genesis 1:1). It now closes with a similarly magnificent declaration, "that God may be all in all" (1 Corinthians 15:28).

The objective of divine revelation, the purpose of the incarnation, the accomplishment of vicarious atonement, and the whole scheme of redemption have been perfectly realized; "God is all in all."

Come, sound His praise abroad,
    And hymns of glory sing;
Jehovah is the sovereign God,
    The universal King.

He formed the deeps unknown;
    He gave the seas their bounds;
The watery worlds are all His own,
    And all the solid ground.

Come, worship at His throne,
    Come bow before the Lord;
We are His work, and not our own,
    He formed us by His Word.

Today attend His voice,
    Nor dare provoke His rod;
Come, like the people of His choice,
    And own your gracious God.

ISAAC WATT

O river of my peace,
Rock of my rest! shelter from every storm!
Light of my darkness, joy of my distress!
Balm of my wounded spirit! morning star
Of all my future! haven of my hopes;

O Dayspring from on high, whose cloudless light
Has beamed upon me—banishing my night
With dawn of Heaven. Sun of righteousness
Rise, oh forever rise! and ever shine
Brighter and brighter! From all weeping eyes
Remove all tears, and over all Thy saints,
And over earth and Heaven, and o'er the bounds
Of time's dark night, and far into the depths
Of eternity pour out the light,
Pour out the sea of glory—inexhaustible.
Pour out forever and forevermore,
And o'er the earth renewed, and azure Heaven
Unshadowed, and the realms of endless peace,
Spread the sweet noontide of the hallowed day
Of God—the sabbath of Eternity.[1]

H. G. GUINNESS

---

[1]In George F. Trench, *After the Thousand Years,* page 117.

BIBLIOGRAPHY

Alford, Henry. *The New Testament for English Readers.* Chicago: Moody Press.

Anderson, Norman. *The Mystery of the Incarnation.* Downers Grove, Illinois: InterVarsity Press.

Barnhouse, Donald Grey. *The Cross Through the Open Tomb.* Grand Rapids: Eerdmans, 1961.

Baron, David. *The Visions and Prophecies of Zechariah.* London: Hebrew Christian Testimony to Israel.

Bellett, John G. *A Short Meditation on the Moral Glory of the Lord Jesus Christ.* London: W.H. Broom, 1865.

Berkouwer, G.C. *The Person of Christ* (Studies in Dogmatics, vol. 4). Grand Rapids: Eerdmans, 1957.

Bettenson, Henry. *The Early Christian Fathers.* New York: Oxford University Press, 1956.

Brooks, W. E. *Jesus is Coming.*

Bruce, F. F., ed. *New International Commentary on the New Testament.* Grand Rapids: Eerdmans.

Bullinger, E.W. *The Companion Bible.* London: Bagster.

Buswell, James Oliver, Jr. *A Systematic Theology of Christian Religion.* Grand Rapids: Zondervan.

Chafer, Lewis Sperry. *Systematic Theology* (vol. 7). Dallas Seminary Press, 1948.

Craig, Samuel G. *Jesus of Yesterday and Today.* Philadelphia: Presbyterian and Reformed.

Edersheim, Alfred. *Jesus the Messiah.* Grand Rapids: Eerdmans, 1954.

Ellicott, Charles J. *Ellicott's Bible Commentary.* Grand Rapids: Zondervan.

Fairbairn, Patrick. *Studies in the Life of Christ.* Grand Rapids: Zondervan.

Farrar, F. W. *The Life of Christ.* London: Cassell and Company, 1892.

Fenton, Ferrar. *The New Testament in Current English.* Islington N., England: J.S. Dodington, (rev. of 1883), n.d.

Fitch, William. *The Beatitudes of Jesus.* Grand Rapids: Eerdmans, 1961.

Fitzwater, Perry B. *Christian Theology: A Systematic Presentation.* Grand Rapids: Eerdmans, 1948.

Grant, F. W. *The Atonement in Type, Prophecy, and Accomplishment.* New York: Loizeaux Brothers, 1888, 1956.

Guillebaud, Harold E. *Why the Cross?* London: InterVarsity Fellowship, 1946, 1957.

Hodge, Archibald Alexander. *The Atonement.* Philadelphia: Presbyterian Board of Publications, 1869.

Hogg, C. F. *What Saith the Scripture?* London: Pickering & Inglis.

Hoste, William. *Studies in Bible Doctrine.* Kilmarnock, Scotland: John Ritchie.

Huegel, F. J. *The Cross of Christ and the Throne of God.* Minneapolis: Bethany Fellowship.

Jamieson, Fausset, and Brown. *Commentary on the Holy Scripture: Critical and Explanatory.* New York: George H. Doran, n.d.

Jennings, F. C. *Studies in Isaiah.* Neptune, New Jersey: Loizeaux Brothers, 1935.

Jukes, Andrew. *The Names of God in Holy Scripture.* London: Longmans, Green, 1889; Grand Rapids: Kregel, 1966.

Kelly, Howard A. *A Scientific Man and the Bible.* Philadelphia: Sunday School Times, 1925.

Kent, Homer A. *The Pastoral Epistles.* Chicago, Moody Press.

Kidner, F. Derek. *Genesis* (Tyndale Old Testament Commentaries). Downers Grove, Illinois: InterVarsity, 1968.

Krummacher, Frederick W. *The Suffering Saviour.* Boston: Gould & Lincoln, 1850; Chicago: Moody Press, 1947.

Lange, John Peter. *Lange's Commentary on the Holy Scriptures* (12 volumes). Grand Rapids: Zondervan.

Liddon, Henry P. *The Divinity of our Lord and Saviour Jesus Christ.* Oxford: Rivingtons, 1875.

Lloyd-Jones, D. Martyn. *Studies in the Sermon on the Mount.* Grand Rapids: Eerdmans.

Machen, John Gresham. *The Virgin Birth of Christ.* New York: Harper, 1930.

McClain, Alva J. *The Greatness of the Kingdom.* Chicago: Moody Press.

Morgan, G. Campbell. *The Teaching of Christ.* New York: Fleming H. Revell, 1913.

______. *The Crises of the Christ.* New York: Fleming H. Revell, 1903.

Morris, Leon. *The Apostolic Preaching of the Cross.* Grand Rapids: Eerdmans, 1955.

Newberry, Thomas. *Solar Light as Illustrating Trinity in Unity.* London: Pickering & Inglis.

Pache, René. *The Return of Jesus Christ.* Chicago: Moody Press, 1955, 1975.

Pape, William H. *The Lordship of Jesus Christ.* Chicago: Moody Press, 1958.

Pentecost, J. Dwight. *Things to Come.* Grand Rapids: Zondervan, 1958.

Pierson, Arthur T. *The Bible and Spiritual Criticism.* New York: Baker & Taylor, 1905.

Ramsay, William M. *The Christ of the Earliest Christians.* Richmond: John Knox Press.

Ryrie, Charles Caldwell. *The Basis of the Premillennial Faith.* Neptune, New Jersey: Loizeaux Brothers, 1953.

Saphir, Adolph. *Christ in the Scriptures.* Kilmarnock, Scotland; John Ritchie, n.d.

Scroggie, W. Graham. *Prophecy and History.* London: Marshall, Morgan & Scott, n.d.

Seiss, Joseph A. *The Gospel in the Stars.* Philadelphia: Muhlenberg Press, 1884; Grand Rapids: Kregel, 1972.

Stalker, James. *The Life of Christ.* New York: Fleming H. Revell, 1889.

Strong, Augustus Hopkins. *Systematic Theology.* Chicago: Judson Press.

Tasker, Randolph V., ed. *Tyndale New Testament Commentaries.* London: Tyndale Press, 1959.

Tatford, Frederick A. *Prophecy's Last Word.* Eastbourne, Sussex: Bible and Advent Testimony Movement.

______. *The Prophet of Messiah's Advent.* Eastbourne, Sussex: Bible and Advent Testimony Movement.

______. *The Prophet of the Myrtle Grove.* Eastbourne, Sussex: Prophetic Witness and Advent Testimony Movement.

Thomas, W. H. Griffiths. *Christianity Is Christ.* Grand Rapids: Eerdmans, 1950.

Trench, George F. *After the Thousand Years.* London: Morgan & Scott, 1894.

Trotter, William. *Plain Papers on Prophetic and Other Subjects.* London: Macintosh, n.d.; New York: Loizeaux Brothers, n.d.

Unger, Merrill F. *Great Neglected Bible Prophecies.* London: G. Morrish, 1865; Chicago: Scripture Press, 1955.

Vincent, M. R. *Word Studies in the New Testament.* MacDonald Publishing Company, (1886).

Walker, Thomas. *The Book of Acts.* Chicago: Moody Press, 1965.

Walvoord, John F. *The Rapture Question.* Grand Rapids: Zondervan, 1970.

______. *The Revelation of Jesus Christ.* Chicago: Moody Press, 1966.

______. *Jesus Christ our Lord.* Chicago: Moody Press.

Warfield, Benjamin Breckinridge. *The Person and Work of Christ.* Philadelphia: Presbyterian and Reformed, 1970.

West, Nathaniel. *The Thousand Years in Both Testaments.* New York: Revell, 1880; Scripture Truth Book Company, n.d.

SCRIPTURE INDEX

MARK

LUKE

EPHESIANS

PHILIPPIANS

COLOSSIANS

1 THESSALONIANS